Trashing Stu

A LOVE STORY & MEMOIR

GRETA EICHEL

To Jennifer,
Keep fashing your
wonderful smile.
Warmly,
Greta

Also by Greta Eichel:
Surviving Ellen
A Memoir

The photo on the cover was taken in 1967 at
Yellowstone National Park. We were on a 7,000-mile
car trip with our seven-year old son, Steven, and
his four-year-old sister, Ellen. Stu was thirty-five. The
photographer was thirty. She had her doubts about
taking the photos in front of the children—setting an
example and so forth. Other tourists circled as far away
from us as was safe, trying to avoid both our family and
their falling off the mountain.

Note: All of the events that take place in this book are true and
all of the people are real. I have changed some of the names, where
their inclusion might cause embarrassment. Parts of some stories
were included in my first book, *Surviving Ellen*.

Illustrations by Stu Eichel
Cover & book design by Greta Eichel

Trashing Stu:

EICHEL ARTISTS
& ASSOCIATES

Praise for Greta Eichel's first book, *Surviving Ellen*

An incredible read. It's beautiful. It flows. I read it in one night.
—Sandy Lesberg / SANDY LESBERG'S WORLD
WOR New York City Radio Critic at large

Surviving Ellen *a masterful story: A heartwarming story of love
and humor in the face of great tragedy, and a wonderful read.
Beautiful and funny, Ellen Eichel killed herself when she was 29.
But though scattered throughout with sadness and indignation,*
Surviving Ellen *reads more like well-told gossip—startling, lively,
and true (Eichel's) remembrances spring off the page and into the
reader's memory.*

—Kathryn Ceceri / THE POST-STAR

Greta Eichel has produced a moving family memoir in her book,
Surviving Ellen. *The title refers to Eichel's daughter, a young
woman who committed suicide. Don't be put off by the suggested
theme: this is a multi-generational story of courage, commitment,
pain, humor, and truth—a story you can draw strength from . . .
a story that makes you laugh, makes you cry, makes you wonder,
and ultimately makes you appreciate and celebrate life.*

—Kim M. Smithgall / THE SARATOGA POST

Greta Eichel's Surviving Ellen *is part autobiography, part
memoir, part eulogy. With unflinching honesty, Eichel searches
her own history for the seeds of her daughter Ellen's suicide and
for signs of life after Ellen's death. With prose so free of artifice
that it becomes a poetry of clarity, with images so sharp they often
hurt, Eichel struggles with heart and conscience as she renders
the ferocious pain of loss . . . this deeply moving, affective
testimony reminds us how the dramatic and the ludicrous are
inextricably tangled in the lives of ordinary people.* Surviving
Ellen *unlocks the secrets of the heart.*

—Allen Wier, author of Tehano / Blanco / A Place for Outlaws /
Things About to Disappear / Departing as Air

*Writing Memoirs brings catharsis, peace: Greta Eichel wrote her
memoir* Surviving Ellen *to cope with her daughter Ellen's suicide.
She gets letters and emails from all over the country. At readings
people can't wait to talk to her. They tell her about their son, their
brother, or their mother who killed themselves. She said it's so
common it's frightening, but there is still a stigma. Yet* Surviving
Ellen *is sprinkled with humor and ends on a high note.*

—Karen Bjornland / THE SUNDAY GAZETTE

To my husband Stu & my
granddaughters Michaela & Jordana

CONTENTS

Acknowledgements

When someone asked my husband, Stu, how he felt about me writing a book called "Trashing Stu," he replied: "Greta doesn't tell me what to paint and I don't tell her what to write." Aside from the fact that we love each other, that simple statement sums up how we have stayed married to each other since 1956.

Thanks to the people in my writer's group, who gave honest, extremely helpful criticism and encouragement: Judy Coburn, Mimi Ciancio, Claudia Doeblin, Marilyn Sandberg, and Alice Zeiger.

Thanks to my friends Sue Carey, Reenie and Hal Ernest, Dee Montie and Murray Evans, Jane Garron, Jim Kelly, Abby and Charles Kleinbaum, Elana Mark, Anna Montgomery, Linda Rosenbluth, Joan and Ron Short, my son Steven, and my daughter-in-law, Michele for your strong support from afar throughout this project. From close-by, thanks go to my friends Ardith Russell, Gloria Arnold, Judith Thomas, and Barbara Kass.

Thanks to Mary Beth D'Aloia for her patient help in both proofreading and solving so many of those plaguing computer mysteries. My great appreciation to Nancy Goldberg for her insightful editing.

I give many thanks to my new friend Bonita Weber and the group of women at the Huron Valley Women's Correctional Facility in Ypsilanti, Michigan. They have declared Friday evening in the dayroom "Greta & Stu Night." Bonita has read aloud to them all the chapters of *Trashing Stu* that I sent her.

I would also like to thank our dentist, Dr. Richard Dunham and his office manager, Suzanne Anderson, for reading these chapters as I went along. I could always hear Suzanne laughing in her office while Dr. Dunham worked on my teeth.

Special thanks go to my ten-year-old granddaughter, Michaela, for saying: "Grandma Greta. I loved reading *Trashing Stu*. You've just *got* to get it published."

Foreword

Well, Greta, your manuscript arrived yesterday accompanied by a note from Stu that said: "I didn't know I was so fucking interesting." He's not! He's fuckin' fascinatin' . . . and even though we already knew that, we have been spellbound by your funny, intensely honest, loving, gifted storytelling. We have all the chapters out of order, of course, because we keep walking by and saying, "Okay, one more and then we have to . . . (fill in the blank)."

Here's the other side of the story: Our friend, whose son was murdered, is visiting for a few days. So your manuscript arrived and Ron and I were interrupting each other trying to explain who you all are and showing him pictures and reading him pieces from the manuscript. He kept asking questions about how we knew you all, etc., and we were answering a mile a minute with funny stories and endearing memories.

In the course of that conversation, we mentioned Ellen and your book, *Surviving Ellen*. He stopped, literally dropped the chapter he was holding onto the table, and tears streamed out of his eyes. "How did they learn to laugh again?" he said. He was so touched by your and Stu's relationship and all the humor in it. He just kept saying, "Will I ever be able to laugh again?"

Love to both of you,
Joan

Joan Boyd Short

GRETA EICHEL

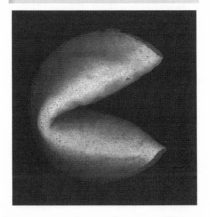

☺ Every man is a volume if you know how to read him. ☺

Introducing Stu

I have always listened to the stories of strangers. Now that I've retired, I'm home much of the time. When workmen come over, I show them Stu's artwork. His paintings and drawings are displayed on every square inch of our walls. I show them to the plumbers, the electricians, the exterminators, and the guys that fix the furnace. Many of them don't feel comfortable in museums and art galleries, but they spend a long time looking very carefully at every piece of art in our house. Sometimes they tell me the story of their lives. Now, after almost six decades of marriage, I've decided to tell Stu's story to strangers. I truly couldn't make any of this up.

Stu Draws

Stu can't remember a time
when he didn't draw.

If you are born with a
silver spoon in your mouth, you
are born into a rich family.

Stu, and his twin brother, Edward, were born with yellow pencils in their hands. It was 1932—the height of the Great Depression. No silver spoons for them.

Their father Martin Eichelbaum, a baker of bread and rolls who, during the Depression couldn't find a job as a baker, drove a cab so he could feed his family. Both boys inherited their mother Elizabeth's artistic genes. A pencil was probably their only toy. Both of them became artists. Neither gave a thought to any other profession.

THE END OF THE DEPRESSION

"When my kindergarten teacher chose my work to go up on the wall, that was it," Stu said. He never once considered becoming a fireman or a cowboy. "Even back then I had a vague notion that I was special because I had artistic talent. This carried me right through high school, where I never felt inferior in spite of being a ninety-nine pound non-athletic wimp."

Martin Eichelbaum, once again a baker when the Depression was over, worked six nights a week making bread and rolls to be delivered the following morning. He slept during the day. If the boys made any noise their father came roaring down the stairs and beat them up. Drawing, a *quiet* activity, was encouraged.

Edward was always more serious about school and behaved in class. Stu was every teacher's nightmare—acting up and playing the class clown. Stu's fifth grade teacher told his parents, "Your boys were cute when they were little, but Stuart isn't cute anymore." Many of his teachers repeatedly summoned Stu's parents to visit the school, even into his high school years, to speak to them about their son's bad behavior.

It was fortunate for our future relationship that Stu and I didn't meet before we were in college. We would have *hated* each other in elementary school. I was always a goody-goody, and the teacher's pet. I would have told someone like Stu to shut up and pay attention to the teacher.

Stu's twin decided to go to Cass Tech in Detroit, one of the best art high schools in America. Stu had planned to go to Central High, which was considered the "social Jewish high school." But, afraid that his brother would learn to draw better than him, Stu decided on going to Cass instead. It was one of the best decisions of his life.

The art students at Cass were also required to take a few very elementary academic courses—Stu received a grade of D- in all of them. "They gave me a passing grade because they didn't want to ever see me again," Stu told me.

THE END OF HIGH SCHOOL

Stu graduated from Cass and took the entrance exam for Wayne State in Detroit. He went off the graph in math—there was nothing low enough to measure him. I believe because Michigan state law required that anyone graduating from high school be admitted to a state college Stu was let into Wayne—on probation. He did miserably in all his academic classes, but didn't drop out of Wayne because he loved having his "Grief Case" cartoons published in the school newspaper.

Two of Stu's cartoons that were published in the Wayne State newspaper.

Stu spelled "junior" wrong, in the cartoon of the boy having just dumped his grandmother out the window, but the editor didn't catch the mistake. The misspelled word, however, wasn't the reason he was kicked off the staff. He had created a "Grief Case" drawing that was considered too far out—even for the school paper. He'd drawn a cartoon of a family sitting around their holiday dinner table with a whole roasted pig in the center. A child is frantically waving his hand saying, "Dibs on the eyeballs." It was probably the final straw.

So Stu dropped out of Wayne State and enrolled in Arts & Crafts in Detroit, which was a two-year school that taught art only. There were no academic classes—Stu's nemesis in High School. He was accepted by Arts and Crafts because he could draw so well, but he quit after six months and joined the army. School was not yet for him.

Korea wasn't for him either, but dropping out was called going AWOL—not an option. Stu made the best of his three years in Korea and Japan and continued drawing. However, the only thing that anyone ever asked him to draw was a picture of people fucking. He always drew what was surely a disappointment to any soldier who had requested it.

A MESSAGE FROM THE PAST

On May 19, 2010, Stu received an email sent from someone he must have known sixty years ago. It was sent to my email address; the subject line said: Are you Stuart Eichelbaum from Detroit?

Dear Stuart,
I have found your letters (if it is you) from Korea
and was wondering if you would like to have
them.
Leah Pollack Wexler

Stu was embarrassed that he had no idea who she was, so he asked me to please answer her email. She had saved Stu's letters from Korea all these years and I was very touched. I wrote that we would love to have the letters. She sent them soon afterwards

Leah and I exchanged emails for a while. When we received the envelope with Stu's crumbling, yellowed airmailed letters from Korea, I insisted Stu write her a letter of thanks. He did. I also wrote to her:

Hi Leah,
We received the letters yesterday and can't thank
you enough for sending them. Both of us loved
reading them. What amazed me was that I didn't
know Stu until after his army days, but he hasn't
changed a bit. The cartoons look like what he
would draw today. His voice has hardly changed.

When Stu was discharged from the army he decided it was time to get serious. He enrolled for the second time as a student at Arts & Crafts in Detroit. He heard from the best student there that Pratt Institute was the top art college in America and decided that was where he wanted to be. I was already there waiting for him.

Stu's Army Daze

Stu was promoted from Private 1st Class
to Corporal after serving for a year in Korea.

*The history of April Fools' Day
sometimes called All Fools' Day
has never been totally clear.*

My husband enlisted in the U.S. Army on April Fools' Day, 1952. The reason Stuart Eichelbaum signed up for three years, instead of waiting to get drafted for two years, was never totally clear to him. The United States was then in its second year of losing, or fighting to a draw, the so-called "Military Action" in Korea—sometimes referred to as "The Forgotten War." He had no idea what it was about. I was surprised to learn that about ten million people died during the Korean War: I wonder how many of them knew what it was about.

Stu speculates that he joined the army to get away from his father, who, when his son left for basic training, wouldn't even say goodbye. Or maybe Stu just wanted to see more of the world than he'd seen when he was growing up in Detroit. He was nineteen and looking for adventure. After his honorable discharge, Stu went to college on the GI Bill.

THE BASICS

The U.S. Army had sent him for basic training to Fort Bliss in El Paso, Texas, where the thermometer rose to 110 degrees during the day and fell below forty degrees at night. The biggest, tallest soldiers sometimes passed out during their daily marches in the desert. At 5' 91/2" tall and weighing 147 pounds, Stu remained upright, thus proving the axiom, "The bigger you are the harder you fall."

In basic training the soldiers were told that their new best friend was their rifle and keeping it clean and ready-to-fire was a priority. They were expected to take their rifles apart, and put them back together in the dark—blindfolded if necessary. Even in the brightest sunlight Stu couldn't complete that task. Once, he lost the rag for cleaning his rifle in the barrel of the gun. He was too embarrassed to admit that he couldn't remove the rag, and would probably have fired the rifle and blown off his head if a fellow soldier hadn't taken it out for him.

My future husband was always getting into trouble and being punished for various infractions of the rules or for being a smartass. He never *could* keep a straight face and, probably because of his bullying father, he had a difficult time with authority figures. "Hit the ground Eichelbaum and give me fifty push-ups," the drill sergeant would scream an inch from Stu's face. "And if you don't wipe that smirk off, you can give me fifty more."

During the ritual of early-morning inspections in the barracks, the soldier who stood directly across from Stu had a way of rolling his eyes back into his head so only the whites could be seen. "Don't laugh until you see the whites of his eyes," may well have been Stu's mantra.

While he stood at attention as the sergeant was inspecting the neatness of his foot locker, the tightness of the sheets on his bunk, the spit-shine on his boots, the perfect knot of his tie, the sharpness of the crease in his pants, the guy facing him would roll his eyes back and Stu would crack up. He would get demerits—just as he did in elementary school—but instead of his parents being summoned to meet with his teachers, he would have to work off his demerits by walking back and forth, back and forth on the drill field for hours on end in the South-Texas heat. The consequences of enlisting in the US Army on April Fools' Day were becoming apparent.

Thinking it would be better to be the officer doing the inspecting rather than the grunt being inspected, Stu took an aptitude test and (amazingly) qualified for Officer Candidates School (OCS). He had to list three choices for the division he wanted to be part of. His first choice was the Signal Corps and his third was Anti-

Aircraft Artillery. Naturally, Stu was granted his third choice—Anti-Aircraft Artillery, which required under-standing math. Stu had always failed math throughout elementary and high school. He flunked out of OCS.

To cover his embarrassment, Stu wrote a letter to his best friend in Detroit saying he had flunked out on purpose, which of course was untrue. An officer who found a ripped-up draft of the letter in the wastebasket where Stu had thrown it, believed he was telling the truth and informed him that the following day he would be shipped out for Korea. Stu was seasick all the way there. For his remaining years in the army he lived in fear of the trip back home.

UNDER THE GUN

Stu was assigned to the K-13 Airbase near the small town of Suwon, south of Seoul, the capital. The airbase was then famous because Ted Williams, the legendary baseball player, had survived the crash-landing of his plane there. Stu spent three months on a large anti-aircraft gun in the rice paddies.

One master sergeant oversaw the four privates who spent most of their day cleaning the gun. The privates were Stu from Detroit, two semi-literate hillbillies from West Virginia, and a black guy from Chicago. The Master Sergeant was a nice guy from St. Louis.

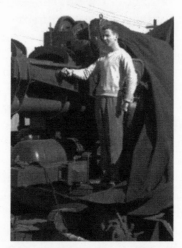

Stu, trying to be funny, poses on the anti-aircraft
gun, looking as miserable as he felt.

Unfortunately for Stu, the other privates on the gun stayed drunk all the time. So several times a night, whenever an airplane flown by either the Chinese or the North Koreans (they never found out which) broke the perimeter of the airbase they were defending. One of them had to fall out and man the gun. The gun did not fire a single shot in the three months Stu was stationed there. The enemy never actually flew *over* the airfield; they were just harassing the troops.

Guard-duty presented another problem. Every night all the privates in his group were required to take turns standing guard for two hours. The privates—except for Stu—were, as usual, dead drunk, passed out and curled up in their sleeping bags, so his turn never ended and he hardly slept at all.

Every night, a soldier who worked in the mess hall traveled by Jeep to the outposts and offered the man standing guard-duty a cup of steaming hot coffee. The nights were bitterly cold and hot coffee really should have been welcome, but Stu detests even the *smell* of coffee and to this day has never swallowed a single mouthful of it. You just didn't say to the guy from the mess hall bearing coffee, "Would you mind bringing me a cup of tea with two sugars and some lemon or some hot chocolate with a lot of whipped cream on top?"

So Stu served his time freezing in the rice paddies every night, having nothing warm to drink, and wishing he were back in Detroit. Even though he had suffered many miserable winters there, he'd never in his life been *that* cold. He felt he was in suspended animation.

After three months on the gun, a chaplain visited the troops to ask if they had anything they wanted to talk about.

"I just want you to know that I'm not deserting," Stu told him. "Tomorrow morning I'm taking my rifle and I'm walking towards the front. Not away from the front. Towards the front, because I'd rather be dead than spend another night on this gun." The following day he was transferred out of K-13 to a headquarters outfit in Seoul, the capital of South Korea.

STU'S MOTHER SENDS COOKIES

The following year he was transferred to an elite army base outside Hiyoshi, Japan, to head a team of Japanese draftsmen who did the math and drew every chart the army used. They were called the "indigenous personnel." Stu's mother, while her son was stationed in Japan, sent him a big box of her homemade oatmeal cookies and enclosed a note telling him to share them with the guys. He offered the Japanese draftsmen, who were extremely shy, some of the cookies. But to a man they declined. Stu left the box of cookies on his desk and left the room. A moment later he thought of something he'd forgotten to take with him. On opening the door, he saw the "indigenous personnel" devouring his mother's oatmeal cookies.

The war in Korea had just ended in a draw. Stu actually enjoyed his year in Japan. Three times a week he went to the USO dances and the Hollywood movies that were shown on the base (with Japanese subtitles).

PLEASE, JUST WALK A STRAIGHT LINE

After three years in the army, Stu was promoted to Sergeant. The only reason he got his stripes was he told the officer who was discharging him that he might re-enlist as a Sergeant, but no way would he come back as a Corporal. So Sergeant Stuart Eichelbaum was told to march the troops onto the ship that was taking them home.

"Come on guys, please just walk in a straight line or something," he asked them nicely. "I have no idea how to march troops." Stu dreaded coming home on the troopship, since he had been so seasick all the way to Korea.

His dread was well founded. He crossed the Pacific from Yokohama, Japan to Seattle, Washington and threw up continually for the entire twelve days at sea. He weighed only 136 pounds when he arrived back in port, having lost eleven pounds. His greatest fear was that he wouldn't be able to sling his duffle bag over his shoulder and walk down the gangplank to get off the ship.

ANOTHER APRIL FOOLS' DAY

On April 1, 1956, exactly four years after the April Fools' Day he had enlisted in the Army, Stu asked me to marry him. I was eighteen, he was twenty-three and we were both enrolled at Pratt. For the next three-and-a-half years until graduation, we lived in the apartment in the basement of my parents' house.

A BAD DREAM

Sometimes, in the middle of the night, Stu woke up in a cold sweat.

"Were you having another bad dream?" I asked.

"Yeah," he said. "I was dreaming I had re-enlisted in the Army, but that *this* time it wasn't a dream."

Forty-three years later, on November 17, 1999 I was watching the nightly news on television. A memorial to the Korean War veterans was just being dedicated in Washington, D.C.

I called out to Stu, "Hurry. Come and watch this. A memorial is being dedicated to your war."

"I don't give a shit about that war," Stu called from another room. "I never knew why I was there and still don't."

Stu's Father

Stu's father must have come straight to the beach from the airport, since he is still wearing a suit jacket and carrying his luggage.

*"Our siblings may be the only people we'll
ever know who truly qualify as partners for life.
Siblings are with us for the whole journey."*

Katherine Conge, Family Sociologist

THE EICHELBAUMS

Stu believed that his father, Martin Eichelbaum, cared more about his own brothers: Moses, Abraham, Solomon, Louis, Milton, Irving, Stanley, and his sister Mary than he did about his own children. Samuel Eichelbaum's nine children, forever bonded by battles with their father and their two stepmothers, thought of themselves as survivors. Mary, their sister, was as fierce in her loyalty to her siblings as any of her brothers. According to Mary, her father's third wife murdered him by pushing him down a flight of stairs.

At this December 27, 1938 wedding of his brother Irving to Vicky Flexer,
Stu's father Martin is second from the right in the middle row.
Stu's grandfather Samuel Eichelbaum, who had three wives, eight sons
and one daughter, sits between the bride and groom.

MARTIN EICHELBAUM

Martin was born January 19, 1908, and grew up in Dover, New Jersey. He came from a family of bakers. His mother succumbed to the influenza epidemic that swept the world in 1918. She died while he was holding her hand. Martin graduated from high school and later became secretary of the baker's union—because he was the only one of all the bakers who could read and write. The eventually infamous union boss, Jimmy Hoffa, was his errand boy. Martin could not find a job as a baker, during the Great Depression, so in 1932 he drove a cab. On June 8th of that year he became the father of twins.

I think Stu's father was simply overwhelmed by the responsibility. The twins' brother, Marvin, was born six years later. On June 8, 1945, when Stuart and Edward were thirteen and celebrating their Bar Mitzvahs, their brother Stanley was born. All four sons worked in their father's kosher-style restaurant and deli, and they all hated it. The Bagel Restaurant & Delicatessen was very successful, but when they grew up, none of the four boys wanted anything to do with the family business.

When we visited Detroit, or when Martin and Stu's mother visited us, Stu's dad talked to me more than he had ever talked to Stu during his entire life. My father-in-law once told me that during the Depression, when the twins were sick, he needed ten cents to buy them medicine. "I didn't have the ten cents," he said, shaking his head sadly.

Stu can't remember his father ever having a conversation with him, hugging him, or telling him that he loved him. He remembers getting beat up by his father. He remembers being humiliated and slapped around in front of customers by his father when he worked in the restaurant. He remembers that his father wouldn't say goodbye to him when he left for the army.

Stu remembers his father as a bully. Martin was 5'8" tall and weighed 250 pounds. He played football in high school and was very strong. He threw drunks that were too rowdy through his restaurant's front door and sometimes the window. Then he kicked them down the street. When he discovered that the Bagel Restaurant & Delicatessen's dishwasher was drinking whiskey on the job, he found the man's bottle hidden away and peed into it.

Martin owned a gun. He picked fights with people—even into his mid-sixties. Stu said his father was the last person on the planet who should ever have a gun. He had a terrible temper and was warned by the Detroit police not to pull his gun on people. Eventually the police took it away from him.

I remember Stu's father differently. The first time I met him was April 17, 1956, when we flew to Detroit for our engagement party. He hugged me and told me he had waited twenty-three years for that day.

Stu's parents also put on our wedding in Detroit. Stu's Aunt Vicky once told me that Stu and I were married on the same day as she and Irving because Stu's parents thought that was a lucky day to marry.

On December 27, 1956, Stu's father dances with me.

Stu and I had no idea when we bought our house in Huntington Station, that one of the Long Island Rail Road crossings was only one-hundred-yards from our bedroom window. Once, while his parents were visiting us, the train blew its long warning whistle. "I *hate* that sound," I said to Stu's dad.

"I *love* that sound," he said softly. "When I was a boy in Dover and I heard that whistle, I thought, *someday I'll be on that train and be out of here.*"

HIS 65TH SURPRISE BIRTHDAY PARTY

On January 19, 1973 Stu's mother gave a surprise party for her husband's sixty-fifth birthday. Stu and I flew in from Tennessee with Steven and Ellen. All of Martin's many friends were there. A good many of his nieces and nephews, who loved their Uncle Martin, attended. Stu told me his dad liked *all* the kids except for his own.

HIS GRANDSON'S BAR MITZVAH

On Thanksgiving in 1972, we visited Stu's parents in Detroit. Our son Steven was then twelve. Jewish boys are supposed to have their bar mitzvah when they are thirteen. "What's the date of Steven's bar mitzvah?" Stu's dad asked.

"Well, we're not part of the Jewish community in Knoxville and we don't plan to bar mitzvah Steven," I said.

"My first grandson is going to have a bar mitzvah," he yelled. It was the first and only time I'd ever seen Stu's father lose his temper. Steven had not gone to Hebrew school and had no training in the complicated rituals of the bar mitzvah.

"Here's what you're going to do," he said slowly. "You will get him a tutor. Steven is very smart and will learn everything he needs to know for his bar mitzvah. The ceremony will be held at our temple in Detroit. I'll invite everyone to the party afterwards and I'll pay for everything. This is very important to me."

It was an offer that he would not allow us to refuse. We had no idea that Martin Eichelbaum cared so much about a Bar Mitzvah. Although I suddenly remembered how upset Stu's parents had been when I had a doctor circumcise their first grandson. I absolutely refused to have a "moehl" (a rabbi that circumcises Jewish baby boys to welcome them into the faith on their eighth day of life) touch my baby.

Nearly two months after we returned to Knoxville, Steven and Ellen received the following letter from Stu's father.

January 19, 1973

Dear Ellen & Steven,

Today is my birthday and it is early morning so I decided to start celebrating by writing to you, which is something I should have done quite some time ago. I have wanted to impress on you, how much I enjoyed this past Thanksgiving Day, when all of you joined Dennis and David and Susan and your Aunt Marilyn and Uncle Marvin, to be with us for the few days. You can be sure your grandma and I enjoyed those few days to a great degree. So much so, that I wish we could see more of you, more often. When we undertook this place of business, I thought we would be able to get away to make visits. But it has not turned out that way.

We have been kept busy and have not been able to get away. Now we are eagerly waiting for your getting here, not too far away, for one of the highlights of our lives. I am referring to your Bar Mitzvah. We hope and expect to have your grandpa and grandma Friedman here for the affair, and also your aunts and uncles, for this is an accomplishment and an occasion.

It was very nice to talk to you during the Christmas holiday. I'm sure it must have been wonderful having your grandma and grandpa with you. Hope school is going along nicely. I feel sure that it is.

Say hello to your mommy and daddy and wish them well. Take care of yourselves, and on this, my birthday, I am a most fortunate person, for all of you.

With love,
Grandpa

We soon hired a tutor who came to our house twice a week for the next six months. He taught Steven just enough Hebrew and whatever he *needed* to know to prepare for his bar mitzvah. We flew to Detroit for the event. Stu's father told us proudly during the party that people from twenty-two different states had come for the celebration.

There were two-hundred-and-fifty people there—as many as came for the wedding he'd given us. I'd never seen him look so happy. Stu's father said to my father: "Now I can die. I've lived to see my first grandson's Bar Mitzvah."

On August 7, 1973, less than three weeks after his first grandson's Bar Mitzvah, Stu's father died from a massive heart attack while working behind the counter in the Bagel Restaurant & Delicatessen. He was just sixty-five. People from twenty-two different states came back to Detroit for his funeral.

Stu Goes to College

Stu decided it was finally
time to get serious.

It was Stu's good fortune
that he was able to receive the
GI Bill. It gave him, and millions of
other veterans, the opportunity to
receive a higher education.

Stu didn't even think he was college material. He'd graduated from high school with only a D- average. But because he had the great advantage of having the GI Bill, he decided he wanted to attend the best art school in America. He thought it would be dramatic if he called the Dean of Pratt Institute's Art School and asked if he could fly in for an interview. The dean said that would be fine. Stu then flew to New York from Detroit with his portfolio in the middle of freshman year. He asked if he could start taking classes immediately. He was twenty-three-years-old.

The Dean looked at Stu's high school record. "Your record is abominable," he said. "However, your portfolio is excellent. We're going to admit you because we like to be good to the GI's. If you can pass the second semester, we'll give you credit for the first." Stu received one A, four B's and two C's in the second semester and was given credit for the first.

ANOTHER VISIT WITH THE DEAN

A month later, the Dean met with Stu once more in his office. Every freshman was required to have a chest x-ray as part of the admissions procedure. Stu went to Brooklyn Hospital, which was near Pratt, and paid the $10 charge in cash. A week later he received a bill for the x-ray. Stu called them and said he had already paid it. The following week he received another bill. He just ignored it. The third bill arrived a week later. Stu called the hospital and said, "I'm going to send back the bill I've already paid. When you receive it, I suggest you stick it up your ass." Some official from the hospital called the Dean to complain about their student's rude behavior. When Stu was summoned to the Dean's office, the Dean laughed and said, "When I was about your age I used to do things just like that." Stu never received another bill.

THE NEW STUDENT

When I started college in September of 1955, I was eighteen and straight out of high school. The class was filled with veterans of the Korean War going to school on the GI Bill. Everyone was extremely serious. It was difficult to get into Pratt, and the competition to stay there was fierce.

I fell in love with Stuart the first time I saw him. Four new students had transferred from other schools for the second half of our freshman year. My future husband was one of them. I didn't know his name yet, or anything else about him, but I knew instantly that he was the man I was going to marry. At the time, I was practically engaged to someone else.

In class each day I studied this man with whom I had fallen in love, but for the first few weeks we hardly spoke to each other. Every morning my father drove me to Pratt Institute, which was in Brooklyn's dangerous Bedford Stuyvesant neighborhood, parked the car and took the subway to work in Manhattan. After work he drove me home to the safety of East Flatbush.

On a cold, blustery, early March day in 1956, Stu was walking to his dorm when I first pointed him out to my father.

"See that guy walking across the street, Daddy?" I said excitedly. "That's the man I'm going to marry."

"What's his name?" my father asked.

"I don't know yet." I said

"He's got a cute ass," my father observed with his usual astuteness.

STU FALLS ASLEEP IN CLASS

In his first week as a student at Pratt, Stu stayed up the entire night to finish the class assignment for two-dimensional design. He arrived late to class, apologized to the teacher, and handed in his creation. He then sat down at a desk at the very back of the class. After listening to the critique of two other students' work, he fell fast asleep. No one yet knew him well enough to wake him up and if the teacher saw him sleeping, she made no comment. When his name was called, he awoke with a start, as if the sound of reveille—the detestable blast of the bugle wake-up call in the army, had just exploded. All of the student's eyes, including mine, were on him. I can still see the beautiful piece he submitted. He had painted two fighters in a boxing ring.

STU MOVES IN

We started dating only a few weeks after I'd pointed Stu out to my father. He lived in the men's dorm, but when we became engaged—three weeks after our first date, Stu moved out the dorm and into the basement apartment of my parents' house.

In late April 1956, my parents, Stu, and I flew from New York to Detroit to meet his family. Stu's parents gave us an engagement party during that first visit, after they realized they couldn't talk their son out of marrying a girl he barely knew. His father sold the car Stu had bought when he was discharged from the army so that his mother could use the money to buy me an engagement ring. We were married eight months later. Everyone in our class probably thought I was pregnant, but we didn't have our first child until more than a year after we graduated.

We subsisted nicely on the $135 that Stu received each month from the GI Bill, the money we made each summer working at various jobs, plus the $75 his parents sent us every month to help out. My parents allowed us live in their basement for free and my mother cooked all of our dinners. I washed and Stu dried the dishes; then we went down to the basement and did our homework until four in the morning. The alarm woke us at six. It wasn't like being married at all, but getting legal permission to sleep together.

Our apartment, was called a "finished basement," and was quite small. The kitchen, in which I never cooked a single meal, had a little pantry that Stu and I turned into a darkroom so we could develop pictures for our photography class. The door allowed light to leak in, so when one of us was developing a photo, the other had to lean against the door as hard as possible to keep the light out.

We slept in a single bed, because there was no way for a double bed to be moved down the tiny, curving stairway. Whenever we had an argument, Stu used to practically paste himself against the wall so we didn't have to touch each other. Our drawing boards were side by side in what could have been a laundry room, but Mother did our laundry as well. Stu and I weren't even *playing* house.

WHAT WE DID ON OUR SUMMER VACATION

Before I met Stu, I had signed a contract for a job as the Art Counselor at beautiful Kee-Wah Camp in the Berkshire Mountains of New York. My mother worked for the camp's owner. I had to be there on the last day of June. After Stu and I became engaged in mid-April, he asked my mother if she could get *him* a job there so we could spend our first summer together.

My mother asked her boss if he could give her future son-in-law a job at Kee-Wah. He hired Stu as a camp counselor. The camp was expensive for the campers, but Stu and I earned only $300 each for the entire summer. It was barely enough to pay for one semester's tuition.

I had never been to camp before, but Stu had been a Boy Scout and slept in a barracks when he was in the army, so he wasn't bothered by the (to me) primitive conditions. I hated camp, hated all the kids, and knew nothing at all about *teaching* art.

Stu loved it. Since he had been a boxer, he taught his campers how to box. Whenever some of the kids in his bunk acted up, he put boxing gloves on them and had them punch each other so that he wouldn't have to. In September we returned to start our sophomore year.

STU FALLS DOWN THE STAIRS

One day, in our junior year, I was summoned from class to the Dean's office where I found Stu lying flat on a wooden bench, his shoe off, his ankle purple and three times its normal size. When he saw me he started to laugh. He couldn't wait to tell me the story of how it happened: On the fifth floor, he'd bet Eli Goldowski, one of our classmates, that he could beat him to the first floor by running down the steps while Eli rode on the ancient elevator. The wonderful, old building was built in 1857 and the stairs were made of marble. After he fell, Stu had to slide down four flights on his butt to get to the first floor.

By the time my father came to pick us up, Stu could barely walk. So, before driving home, we stopped at our family doctor. My father and I sat in the waiting room until Stu eventually joined us. He limped out, with his ankle taped up. It seemed he would actually survive losing the race to Goldowski—his ankle wasn't broken, just badly bruised. My mother even kept dinner warm for us.

STU'S NEMESIS SLAIN AT LAST

Academic subjects were never Stu's strong suit and he was terrified of failing the course he had to take during his first semester at Pratt. Stu studied like crazy and received a B, his first in any class that wasn't an art class; probably because it was the first time he'd ever studied. After choosing our major (We both chose Advertising Design) we then had to take two academic courses each semester in order to receive our Bachelor's Degrees when we graduated.

Stu did not get to Pratt in time to take English with the rest of our classmates. So in his sophomore year, he joined a class in the College of Engineering.

The engineering students couldn't write an English sentence. Amazingly, everyone failed but Stu, who received a "C" as his final grade. However, he received an "A" for a paper he wrote titled, "The Laugh that Lost." It was about the punishment he'd received in Officer's Candidate School for laughing at the most inopportune moments. He'd learned how to do a lot of push-ups and practice salutes.

SOME THINGS AREN'T FUNNY

Three-dimensional design was in fact the only non-academic class in which I received higher grades than Stu. The 3-D professor would place all the students' constructions, from best to worst, on long shelves that were on three sides of the classroom. Once, when Stu's submission was selected, he thought his wire sculpture of a fish was chosen as the best. Wrong.

I was quite good. I was asked to bring my Plexiglas sculpture back the next semester for Pratt's permanent collection—a great honor. On the last day of school, I very carefully put my creation on the floor in the back of my father's car. Stu and I usually sat together in the back, but because my sculpture was on the floor I sat next to my father. Suddenly, my dad slammed on the brakes for a red light; the apparently broken seat-latch allowed my seat to jolt backwards, entirely demolishing my sculpture. I was devastated, but Stu couldn't stop laughing.

I didn't speak to him for days. He finally made me laugh by wearing the button (see below) on his shirt at dinner in my parent's dining room. He'd replaced the furniture salesman's name with "Llama Doody." To this day, I don't know why it struck me as so funny or even why I still have it.

Left: Stu's button Right: Graduation Day / June 5, 1959

Left to right: Stu & me, my mother & father.

SENIORS

During our senior year, Stu and I took a trip to West Point on the "Hudson River Day Line" with my parents. Maybe the reason Stu looks so glum in the above photo is because it was the first time since his discharge from the army that he was that close to anything military or once again finding himself trapped on a boat.

Our entire senior year at Pratt seemed to fly by. Stu graduated with me in 1959, fourth in a class of fifty-two (I was fifth). In the final semester, Stu received five A's, two of which were in the academic classes—a first in his life. Now we are senior citizens and I still have our transcripts. On a shelf in our bedroom closet are the Bachelor of Fine Arts degrees we never framed.

The only class that Stu and I have no memory of at Pratt is painting. Neither of us was at all interested in learning to paint. The irony is that Stu, when he was fifty-nine years old, went back to college as a freshman art student at the University of Tennessee. Now, almost twenty years later, he is a full-time painter.

Stu Drives

I feed Stu a piece of cake, while his mother
(far right) laughs. A while later, we drove
to Windsor, Canada for our wedding night.
It was not a piece of cake.

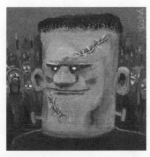

*"The Tunnel of Love is a carnival ride
that takes couples through dark passages.
There are two major themes: a relaxing romantic
ride encouraging the couple to cuddle,
or a spooky horror ride encouraging the couple
to cling to one another."*

Author unknown

HARDLY THE TUNNEL OF LOVE

The night of our wedding was the first time that I sat in the passenger seat while Stu drove. The following morning we got stuck in the tunnel between Windsor, Canada and Detroit, Michigan. Stu's mother had let us borrow her car to drive to Windsor for our wedding night. It seemed very romantic to go to another *country* as Mrs. Stuart Eichelbaum. Greta Friedman had hardly ever been out of Brooklyn.

OUR WEDDING NIGHT

We were married on December 27, 1956, a freezing Thursday night during our Christmas vacation from Pratt Institute. Stu's parents made the wedding, so all my parents and I had to do was buy my dress and fly to Detroit. My parents couldn't afford a large wedding— also the Friedman family was tiny and the Eichelbaum family was enormous. There were 250 people at our wedding. I had five relatives attend plus my best friend Barbara Tobias, who was my maid of honor.

A soon-to-be-heavy snowstorm had started during that dark December afternoon, but Detroiters are used to that. After the wedding and a short drive to Windsor, Canada, Mr. and Mrs. Stuart Eichelbaum checked into the Prince Edward Hotel. While carrying me over the threshold Stu saw the bed and, only then, realized that he had forgotten to bring condoms. Stu wanted to make love on our wedding night, even though we'd been doing it in my parents' basement since our third date.

Since birth control was then illegal in Canada, he had to drive once again through the tunnel to Detroit during the continuing snowstorm, to buy "rubbers"—as they were called back then. By the time he returned I was fast asleep and he didn't wake me up. It had been a very long day.

THE MORNING AFTER

As we drove back to Detroit to pick up my parents and fly home to New York, Stu's mother's car stopped dead in the Windsor/Detroit tunnel. We waited for forty minutes in front of a crowded bus until the tow-truck arrived. The bus was unable to pass us in the narrow, two-lane tunnel.

I watched while my husband-of-one-day got out and kicked the shit out of his mother's car. It turned out the gas-pedal had somehow become disconnected. The pedal was reconnected at a service station; we picked up my parents, took a taxi to the airport and boarded the plane with less than a minute to spare. Stu was still in a terrible mood.

When we got to LaGuardia Airport, my father's 1937 Chevy, which had been parked for three days, started right up. My father then drove us to the Astor Hotel in Manhattan where we spent our four-day honeymoon. It was our first New Year's Eve together.

THE HONEYMOON WAS OVER

On the first day of January 1957, my father picked us up in front of the Astor Hotel and drove us back to Brooklyn. Christmas vacation was over and it was time for us to go back to school and complete our sophomore year.

Stu and I bought our first car in 1960, the year our son Steven was born and we'd moved out of my parents' basement to another basement apartment five blocks away. We bought a Plymouth Valiant, and drove that car for the following nine years. In 1969 we purchased a Ford Fairlane and drove to Knoxville, Tennessee, where we lived for the next thirty years. In 2000 we moved to Saratoga Springs, New York, driving our 1996 Honda. Amazingly, after all these years, Stu has only had a few minor automobile accidents.

DRIVING LESSONS

Stu's mother had taught him how to drive. She was the worst driver I've ever seen—even worse than Stu. Both she and her son brought out the white-knuckle-terror in any passenger who drove with either of them at the wheel. A friend of mine once said that Stu's car had two speeds—off and on. Stu told me his mother was well known to all the Detroit cops and had been ticketed more times than she would say.

When Stu was eighteen he was stopped by a Detroit cop for driving down a one-way street in the wrong direction. The policeman looked at Stu's driver's license and asked, "Who taught you how to drive?"

"My mother," Stu answered. The officer rechecked the last name on Stu's license and let him go without giving him a ticket. The Eichelbaum family was already doing more than their share in supporting Detroit.

Our 2012 Christmas card, illustrated by Stu, said:
"Santa can scare the shit out of you."
So can being a passenger when driving
with either Stu or his mother.

40

Stu tried to teach me how to drive when I was twenty-seven and we'd moved to the suburbs, but I fired him after just one lesson. To save our marriage, I hired a certified driving instructor.

I taught our son to drive and Steven taught Ellen. Neither child wanted their father to teach them to drive, since they'd spent their childhoods as passengers in his car.

When Steven was grown and came to visit us, he often said, "Hey Dad, why don't you let me drive?"

"No, that's OK. I'll drive," Stu always answered. Although we are Jewish, I used to see Steven make the sign of the cross before getting into the back seat.

STU SPEEDS

Stu doesn't speed on purpose; honestly, his mind is often elsewhere and he forgets to check to see how fast he's going. The time, he *did* check the speedometer I was, as usual, backseat driving. I'd asked him to please slow down and he told me he was fine.

"I'm only going forty-five miles an hour," he said.

"You can't be going forty-five when you're passing every other car on the Interstate," I said. We pulled into the nearest rest stop and realized our Saturn's entire electrical system had failed and that *nothing,* including the speedometer, was functioning.

During the five years—from 1973 to 1978—that Stu was on the road selling prints of his pencil drawings, he received more speeding tickets than he cared to count. The first year he was given at least twenty in fifteen different states. During the next four years he stopped counting. If there had been a national database at that time checking driver's records, Stu probably would have had his license revoked or possibly been executed.

He was given two speeding tickets the *same day* on the Alcoa Highway in Knoxville—less than three miles from our house. Our auto insurance was then cancelled. After that we were lucky to even locate a "high-risk" insurance program *willing* to insure us. The policy cost a small fortune.

Stu once gave the finger to a cop in an unmarked car that had pulled up next to him while he was probably speeding. The driver kept looking in his window and he assumed the man was gay and trying to pick him up. Stu soon learned that using an obscene gesture to an officer of the law is also a ticket-able offence.

Stu's speeding problems seemed to stop in 1983, when we bought a new Subaru that was equipped with our first cruise control. However, on our way to Detroit just before getting close to Lexington, Kentucky on I-75, we saw the flashing blue lights and were pulled over at 2:00 o'clock in the morning. When the officer shined his flashlight into the rolled down window, Stu screamed,

"You can't say I was speeding. I have cruise control."

"But you ain't got no lights!" said the Kentucky cop.

PROBLEMS WITH HEADLIGHTS

Stu was ticketed in our first car, a 1960 Valiant. We were pulled over on the Long Island Expressway for having the lights on high beam. Stu told the cop it was his first car and he thought that the little blue light, pointed out by the officer indicating that the "brights" were on, was only for decoration. The cop didn't buy it. Actually, Stu did think that. Usually, unless he's on a pitch-dark road, Stu forgets to turn on the lights at all. He believes that if he can see you than you can see him.

My favorite story about Stu's getting pulled over by a cop for a problem with his headlights was only a few years ago. It was the day he'd participated in a "Paint-Out" in Rye, New York. Every year the Rye Art Center hosts a fund-raising event where fifty artists are invited to take part. By eight in the morning they were required to start a painting of anything in the city of Rye or it's environs, finish and frame their painting by four in the afternoon, and stay for the reception that evening where the paintings would be displayed and then sold at auction. (50% of the sale goes to the artist.)

I suggested that he drive to Rye the night before the Paint-Out and stay in a motel so that he would be fresh the following morning. Stu said that he'd decided to get up at 4:00 AM and drive the three hours to Rye. It would be his first "Paint-Out" and he was very excited to take part.

He arrived at Rye with time to spare; finished his painting; framed it and stayed for the reception and auction. He called at 8:30 that evening and told me his painting had sold for the highest price of all, plus he had met a friend from Pratt whom he hadn't seen in almost fifty years. He said he'd be home around 11:30.

At 10:30 the phone rang again. Stu told me when he saw the exit for Mystic Connecticut he figured he must have been going in the wrong direction. When he saw the sign "Welcome to Rhode Island" he knew he was lost. He tried to find a motel close by, because even *he* was tired, but there was not a place to be found. There wasn't even one gas station open and he was running on empty. I wished him luck and tried to sleep, but I was listening for some sound indicating that he had arrived home safely. I was still awake at 4:30 in the morning, when I heard the door open. Since I wasn't sleeping anyway, Stu told me the following story:

"I was out of gas and really too tired to drive. So I pulled into a closed strip mall and slept for half-an-hour. When I woke up I saw a police car nearby. I told the cop I was lost and asked him how I could get back to Albany and where could I buy gas?"

"You're lucky," he said, "You're just a mile from I-91. There's an all-night service station there. Take it North and you'll eventually connect with I-90."

Stu thanked a cop for the first time in his life. He filled up with gas and as soon as he pulled onto I-91 North he saw the flashing blue lights behind him and was pulled over.

"Were you flicking your lights on and off?" the officer asked.

"I don't think so," answered Stu. He actually didn't know if his lights were on or off.

"I'd better check them to see if your lights are even working," said the cop pleasantly, as he reached inside the car. Then he said in a very different tone of voice, "I want you to get out of the car, put your hands on the hood and don't look at me," Stu did as he was told, having no idea what the problem was.

"Did someone bash in your head? You've got blood all over your forehead!"

So Stu explained to the cop that it wasn't blood, but red paint. He told the policeman he was an artist and had just done a painting for a fundraiser at the Rye Art Center. (Our friend from Pratt had already told him he had paint on his head at the auction, but Stu said he'd have to wait till he got home to shower.) The cop said, "I'll buy that. Drive home carefully and get some sleep."

When he arrived home at about four-thirty in the morning, Stu fell into bed wearing all his clothes.

READING WHILE DRIVING

A highway patrolman in Georgia once stopped Stu when he was reading a roadmap while he was driving. The officer asked, "Do you have any idea how fast you were going?" Stu told me he'd said: "How could I know? I was reading," but in reality, Stu the Yankee said, "No sir," to the burly Georgia cop.

"You were going ninety-six miles an hour," said the highway patrolman. "I want you to follow me to court." The Georgia judge said the fine was $150. Stu told him he didn't have that kind of money with him. The judge didn't even look up when he said to the cop, "Put him in jail."

"Let me check my wallet again," said the chastened Yankee while he pulled out every dollar he had.

STU CAN READ

Stu is a voracious reader but occasionally is asked, "Can't you *read?*" That question is often asked by me, sometimes by others. Did I mention that Stu is a runner? Once, on his way to running in a six-mile race in Schenectady, Stu mistakenly put diesel fuel in his non-diesel Honda. His car made a growling noise, slowed to a stop and refused to go any further. While his dead car waited on the sidelines, Stu finished the 10K race and afterward had to be towed by AAA to a nearby service station.

Stu insisted there was no way to know what kind of gas he was pumping; self-service has many drawbacks. I couldn't believe that there wasn't a sign on the pump that said "diesel." To prove to me that he was right, the following day we drove to the offending gas station and Stu said, "See?" "Yes," I replied. "It says DIESEL on the pump as big as life! Can't you read?"

CHASING THE TRAIN

The very first time I witnessed someone asking Stu if he could read I was sitting in the passenger/death seat and gritting my teeth. We were traveling in the Southwest. Off Interstate-40, a Santa Fé train flashed by, pulled by a beautiful, old orange locomotive. In spite of being petrified, I must now admit, the locomotive was gorgeous. Stu wanted to one day use the photograph to create a painting.

Stu chased the speeding train, driving almost 100 miles an hour while I shouted, "It's gone. Forget about it." Stu ignored me and actually caught up with the train, passed it and pulled onto a side road next to the Interstate. But by the time he got out of the car, the locomotive had whizzed past—just out of range while he clicked his camera.

Stu then drove on the side road, hoping to get back on I-40 and catch up with the train. But we had to wait almost twenty minutes while roadwork was being done before a truck showed up that displayed a sign that said in huge type, "FOLLOW ME".

By that time I was no longer speaking to Stu. He passed the truck and drove on the newly paved road until the truck driver sped up, pulled right in front of us, stopped and approached our car shaking his fist.

"Can't you *read?*" the driver said furiously. "You've just ruined a newly paved road, you moron, and now you've got fresh tar all over your car."

I was still not speaking to my husband, but the "follow-me-truck-driver" had said it all. Stu got out of the car and saw that there was black tar all over our white Honda. He then had the gall to ask the truck driver how to get the tar removed, which was quickly hardening on the shiny white surface. The driver, with a pitying look, actually told Stu to get off at the next exit, where there was a truck wash, and the water was hot enough to remove the tar. It cost $60.00 and was worth every cent. Stu still mourns for the missed orange locomotive that he was dying to paint.

BEYOND FEAR

More than fifty years ago we flew to Detroit to visit Stu's family while an ice storm was developing. By the time we landed, sleet and ice covered everything. The plane practically slid off the runway.

Unbelievably, Stu's mother was there to pick us up at Willow Run Airport. Driving back to Detroit, her car skidded and slid while she drove faster than she should have. It was terrifying. I vowed that if I lived I would never be a passenger in her car again. Now, after more than fifty years of sitting in the passenger seat beside Stu, I am beyond fear. Zoloft helps.

Stu Plays to Win

Top left: Stu's twin brother, Edward,
protests after Stu draws a line in the sand.
Top right: Edward—the agony of defeat.
Above: Stu—the thrill of victory.

*A sore loser refers to one who does
not take defeat well, whereas a good sport
means being a "good winner" as well
as being a "good loser."*
Author unknown

Stu is neither a good winner nor a good loser. When he loses, his bad temper erupts. It is not a pretty sight. Whether in sports, cards, or any other game, he *always* plays to win, and it doesn't matter to him at *all* who his opponent is. When our daughter was five years old and she trounced him in that dumb card game, Old Maid, he accused her of cheating. She probably was, but who cared? Playing cards was never Stu's strong suit anyway. He was a champion runner, a very good boxer, but only a fair-to-middling tennis player. And I'm being *kind* when I say that.

TENNIS ANYONE? ANYONE?

My father was a good sport. He was practically the only person willing to play tennis with Stu more than once during all the years we lived in New York. He just tolerated or simply ignored his son-in-law's tantrums.

After Stu and I moved to Tennessee we joined the Knoxville Racquet Club, where usually, polite southern hospitality replaced overt northern hostility, in spite of the fact that Stu's reputation for poor sportsmanship continued undiminished.

Stu once bought an expensive graphite racquet. He told me his old one didn't work. I didn't remind him that it usually didn't. The first day he used it, Stu brought both his new and his old racquets to a match with his unbelievably tolerant friend, Mike. Stu kept switching the new racquet with the old one to see if it would make a difference in his game. When he missed an easy shot he smashed the offending racquet into the fence.

Stu obviously thought it was the old one and good riddance to it. When he realized it was the expensive graphite one, he smacked himself in the head several times and shouted furiously at the sky, "I just destroyed my new racquet."

"Oh Stu. That's a real shame," Mike said with great sincerity. Stu told me later in the day that if *Mike* had done something that stupid in front of *him*, he wouldn't have been able to stop laughing.

HITTING BACK

Stu always loved sports, but didn't weigh enough to play football, was too short for basketball and wasn't fast enough for track. At fifteen he learned to box at a Detroit gym and continued boxing for the next eight years. All through Stu's childhood his father slapped him around and bullied him. Even if it was only in his own mind, Stu needed to think that he would be able to hit him back if his father ever punched him again.

After Stu and I became engaged, my parents said it would be okay with them for my fiancé to live in their basement apartment. One night, walking home from a movie, Stu asked if I'd ever seen the movie "One Million B.C." I told him I'd never even heard of it. Stu was eight-years-old in 1940 when the film came out, and he never forgot it. I was only three in 1940 and had not yet seen my first movie. "What was it about?" I asked.

"Well, it takes place in prehistoric times. There are only two tribes; one is brutal and the other one gentle. It's about this guy that's a member of the aggressive tribe who's banished from his people for defying his father. He wanders around the jungle and is adopted by the more civilized tribe."

"You know," said Stu, "when I moved in with your folks I felt like I had left the brutal tribe for the gentle tribe."

A GOOD LEFT JAB

Stu once sparred at the gym with Detroit's Lester Felton. For those of you lucky enough never to have heard of him, Felton was ranked the #1 Contender for the "Welterweight Championship of the World." Since Stu was the only boxer to show up at the gym on the day Felton was working out, the coach asked him if he'd mind sparring three rounds with Lester.

Stu was thrilled. Felton promptly knocked the wind out of him with a good left jab. When Stu came back to his corner after the first round ended, his coach said,

"I'll bet you thought Lester hit you with a big right hand." Stu then replied "No, I thought he hit me with a baseball bat." Stu danced away from Felton for the entire second round and was not even insulted when his coach took him out before the third. He had actually sparred with the man who had once *beaten* Kid Gavelin, the Welterweight Champion of the World,

In the Army Stu boxed in Korea and Japan. In a match held on his base in Japan, Stu beat an ex-football-player who weighed fifteen pounds more than he did. After the match his opponent said he was glad he'd played football and would never box again.

Stu throws a left jab at the ex-football-player and soon-to-be-ex-boxer.

When we lived in my parents' basement, I saw Stu shadow boxing for the first time. Shadow boxing is sparring with an imaginary opponent when training for a match or just keeping yourself in shape in case you ever need to punch someone. I was totally awed by the speed and power of Stu's left jab. I watched as he danced around his imaginary opponent, throwing right crosses and left jabs and combinations of both. The odd thing was that it didn't even seem silly doing something that should have looked ridiculous—punching the air. Boxers are trained to visualize their opponent. Now I can't help wondering if Stu wasn't punching his father's shadow.

I hadn't seen Stu shadow box for thirty years. but on June 8, 2012, his 80th birthday, I came downstairs to give him his birthday present (three pairs of running shorts) and saw him shadow boxing in the living room. He looked almost embarrassed when I walked in.

COMPETING WITH GRETA

Stu is fiercely competitive in *whatever* he's doing. Truthfully, so am I. When he and I were art students at Pratt Institute we started a lifetime of competing with each other. Stu's sense of competition is always in high gear, visible to everyone. My competitive drive is mostly in low gear. I try *not* to show how much I care about winning.

Stu and I were together in all of our classes. Our Two-Dimensional-Design professor once compared our work during a critique, displaying them side-by-side. "Your wife beat you out today Mr. Eichelbaum," he said. I inwardly gloated; Stu visibly winced. Luckily for our marriage, that rarely happened. In *Three*-Dimensional Design though, I was excellent and Stu was awful.

Living in my parents' basement apartment was like playing house. My mother always cooked dinner and even did our laundry. The only household chore I had to do was wash the dishes after dinner. Stu dried. We then went down to our side-by-side drawing boards and worked on our homework assignments until the wee hours of the morning.

To take a break, Stu and I conducted our own Gin Rummy tournament. We decided that whoever got to 5,000 points first would win. After about a year, when I was within 30 points of victory, Stu "knocked" with 14 points. Anyone who has ever wasted their time playing Gin Rummy knows you can only knock with 10 points or less. Stu insisted he knew the rules. We ended our tournament in a draw. He wasn't even close.

When I became pregnant with Steven two weeks after I started my first job, we moved out of my parents' basement apartment to our own basement apartment five blocks away. I continued working until the end of my eighth month.

Stu's cousin Arnold gave us a tabletop hockey game for a "house warming" gift. It was about four feet long and two feet wide. You played by manipulating knobs on each end that controlled little cutout metallic hockey players, moving them quickly enough to block the puck and eventually score a goal. Stu was terrible, although he did win once or twice. Pure luck.

We kept the hockey game set up on the coffee table in our apartment and played every night after dinner. By the time I was in my 7th month, ninety-six- pound me had gained almost thirty pounds and I could barely get close enough to reach the hockey players' knobs. Stu nagged me into playing tabletop hockey until I was in the middle of my 9th month. By then I'd gained a grand total of forty-one pounds, so he foolishly thought he might have a chance to win another game. But he never did.

STU COMPETES WITH STEVEN

When Steven was three I taught him to play the game Concentration. It involved turning all the cards in a deck face down, then turning them up two at a time; if they matched, you kept them. Whoever wound up with the most cards won. You had to concentrate very hard and remember where the cards were.

Steven has had an almost photographic memory since early childhood. He usually beat me and *always* beat his father at Concentration. One time, by some insane fluke when Steven was four years old, Stu beat him playing Concentration. Steven ran into his room, throwing himself on his bed and crying. I asked him what had happened. He choked out: "Daddy beat me at Concentration."

"Now Steven, you have to learn that sometimes you win and sometimes you lose. That's life." He stopped crying just long enough to tell me that he already knew that. "But did Daddy have to say, Ha, ha, ha, I trounced the kid? "

When Steven was five-years-old and Ellen was two, we lived in Huntington Station. Before we went to sleep one Friday night in the winter of 1965, the snow had started to fall. By the time we woke up, eighteen inches covered the ground. Stu, Steven, and Ellen went outside to build a snowman. I watched them from the kitchen window while I made a hot lunch.

Ellen helped her father to create a huge snowman masterpiece. Steven, never a team player, struggled to build his own. After an hour of intense effort, Steven came storming into the house, crying. I asked him what happened. "Daddy said that my snowman looks like his snowman's dog."

Stu received only one tennis trophy in his life—for losing in the first round of a tournament, The trophy was a joke: it showed a tennis player without a racquet. Steven has won many trophies with players holding a tennis racquet. After a short time, he won *every* tennis match he played against his father. Stu then took up running.

STU RUNS

Stu hadn't run fast enough to make the track team in high school and didn't try running again until he joined the army, where he then became a member of a championship track team.

After getting out of the army, Stu didn't race again for the next twenty-five years. Almost a decade after we moved to Tennessee, he took up competitive running once again. According to the *Knoxville News Sentinel*, Stu became, "A Legend In His Own Time." He won his age group more than 400 times.

After Stu wins, he shows no mercy and needles the next man crossing the finish line, "Are you coming in last today or first in next week's race?"

In 1995 Stu and Steven competed in the same race on Cape Cod. Stu, sixty-three, won first place in his age category. Steven, who was thirty-five had a much faster time (even though he'd forgotten to bring his racing shoes), but he didn't win anything.

Children never really forget. When Steven got back to Boston, he sent us the following note:

Dear Mom and Dad:

Thanks for a very nice weekend. Although Dad's time was slower than my snowman's dog could run, I can see that once I wear my racing shoes, we'll have to go to the races in separate cars since I won't be able to stand around until Dad finishes.

Okay, enough childish taunting! I realize that "He of few running trophies must tread lightly. Did Confucius or Goethe say that?

Love, Steven

STILL RUNNING

Stu presently runs six miles every other day and continues running with the Saratoga Stryders every Saturday morning. Only four months short of his 80th Birthday, he decided to give up running ten miles every Sunday. The decision was made when I looked out the window and saw Stu returning from his Sunday run.

When he came to the door I asked him if he was doing his usual Hunchback of Notre Dame imitation to amuse the neighbors or if he was crippled. "The latter," he replied as he staggered into the house. Ever since Stu had first started running he always appeared to be in *agony*. I had told our neighbors in the past not to call 911—that Stu just *looks* like he's about to die. I may have to rethink that one.

STILL PUNCHING

Stu was angry when he caught his finger in the door of our relatively new refrigerator, a Kenmore Elite. The exterior is of 'brushed' stainless steel so as not to show fingerprints. He had hit the freezer door with a good left jab. The dent, which I didn't notice all day, caught my eye while we were having dinner at our kitchen table. With the light on, it stuck out like a sore thumb.

"What happened to the refrigerator?" I asked Stu, who pretended he didn't hear me—a typical ploy of men married to Jewish women. I waited.

"I punched it," he eventually replied, as if that was his final answer to a dumb question.

"What did it do?" seemed like the next logical thing to ask.

"It caught my finger," he said.

Punching stainless steel must have hurt, but I didn't ask. After all, when we bought it I *had* said, "I guess this will be our last refrigerator." I think Stu just didn't want to lose a fight with that Kenmore, who would be with us for the rest of our lives.

"Well, you showed it not to fuck with Stu Eichel," I said.

To lovingly remind him not to smack it again, I used a heart magnet to cover the dent and an arrow magnet to point it out.

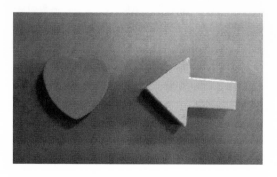

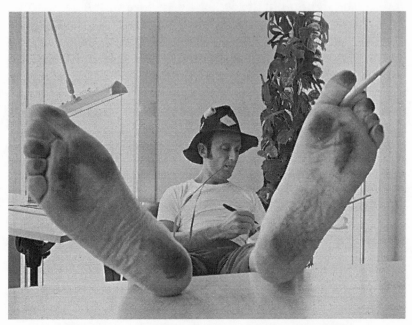

Stu Goes South

Stu gets into the spirit of living in Tennessee
on his first day as Creative Director
of Lavidge & Associates.

*Stu never liked living In New York.
Whenever I said, "Hurry up or
we'll miss our train" he'd answer,
"If it's our train, it will wait for us."*

At the end of May in 1969, a classified ad changed our lives forever. I was thumbing through *Advertising Age,* a trade publication I rarely read, when the ad caught my eye. It said: "Wanted: Art Director. How would you like to live ten minutes from the office, half an hour from the Great Smoky Mountains, and work for one of the Southeast's best advertising agencies?"

We had lived in Huntington Station for four years and Stu spent three hours a day commuting to and from Manhattan. Since graduating from Pratt Institute ten years before, he had worked as an art director on Madison Avenue and had recently been fired by the large advertising agency that had employed him for the last five years. It was nothing personal. They fired his whole group. (He won't even watch the program Admen on TV because it hits too close to home.)

It took several months for Stu to find his next job as an art director. It was for a pharmaceutical company and he was not the least bit interested in advertising pharmaceuticals; at the time though, there weren't a lot of choices.

Stu had always possessed the talent, but he never had the type of personality it took to survive as an adman in New York. If he had, I probably wouldn't have loved him. Stu could never be just another rat in the race. He was actually fired from three different jobs for laughing at the boss.

A LETTER TO LAVIDGE

So when I saw the ad about living ten minutes from the office and near the Great Smoky Mountains—we often headed for mountains on our vacations—I wrote a note with some brief information to Arthur Lavidge, president of Lavidge & Associates. When Stu got home from work, pissed off and exhausted as usual, I told him I had written a letter from him to an advertising agency in Knoxville, and that he should sign his name to it. I put a pen in his hand and pointed to the spot. He signed it without even looking at the letter.

Stu received a response from Arthur Lavidge asking for some more information: where had he gone to school, where had he worked, what had he done, what did he read, where had he traveled, what were his strengths and weaknesses, and why did he want to leave New York. I answered the letter immediately and responded to the questions Mr. Lavidge asked—except for one.

When Stu came home that night, I told him that he had gotten a response to his letter from Lavidge and Associates, that agency in Knoxville to which he had signed his name. He remembered nothing at all about it. So I told Stu that I was now writing another letter with answers to the questions Mr. Lavidge had asked.

"I wrote down your greatest strengths, but he also wanted to know your greatest weakness, and I don't want to tell him you're crazy," I said.

Stu barely glanced up from reading the newspaper. He said to say that his greatest weakness is strawberry shortcake. I thought that was the best line in the letter, which he once again signed, but didn't read. Also asked for were samples of his work, so I told Stu to choose a few pieces from his portfolio that he could send along with his résumé and the unread letter. He did it, but I think he was simply humoring me.

However, I just *knew* that job was his. Stu received a second letter from Art Lavidge, saying that although he had applied for the job of art director, would he be interested in being the creative director of the agency. The creative director is in charge of all the creative departments of an agency—both the art *and* the copy. It was a huge step up and the chance of a lifetime.

STU VISITS KNOXVILLE

The next day, a Saturday, Stu flew to Knoxville. When he got there, as he left the plane, he had to ask the stewardess which state he was in. She told him he was in Tennessee. Stu met with some of the people at the agency, got a tour of the facility and the city, and was offered the job. He told Art Lavidge he'd have to talk it over with his wife. Sunday, he called me.

"The job is mine if we want it. The agency looks great, the people are very nice, the work is good but they can use my help, the city is in a beautiful area, the money is right, but I don't think I can take it," he said.

"Why not?" I asked.

"Because all they talk about is that fucking letter, and I didn't even *read* it." Stu then told me that Art Lavidge had taken him to the Cherokee Country Club for lunch, and when it was time for dessert, had poked him in the ribs with his elbow and said, "How about some *strawberry shortcake*?" Stu thought that Arthur Lavidge might be nuts, but I reminded him that I had written Mr. Lavidge that strawberry shortcake was his greatest weakness.

"Take the job," I said. "We just won't ever tell them who wrote the letter. It isn't dishonest. It was all about you, and you did write the most memorable line."

On Monday, Stu quit his job at the pharmaceutical company, and the next weekend we flew to Knoxville so that I could see the city and meet the people Stu would be working with. We looked for a house and found one that we loved. I flew back to New York, put our house up for sale and sold it to the first people who came to look at it.

Stu stayed in Knoxville to start working. He would be there without us for a month. He wrote me a letter that included photos he'd taken of our new house from every possible angle and also our new mailing address. I wrote Stu: "Steven said he didn't know if he could hold out till the next weekend when you'll be back. He really misses you and Ellen has been walking around holding and hugging that ugly doll. Even the dog seems depressed and just sits in the corner chewing her chewy bone. I miss you too."

Stu came back to Huntington Station a month later for a party I gave to say good-bye to our friends. Before we moved south we had our last name legally changed from Eichelbaum to Eichel. We thought it would be hard enough for our children to be the only Jewish kids in Mount Olive Elementary School. When Stu told Art Lavidge about our name-change he said, "There goes my liberal image."

Lavidge & Associates at night.

Stu rented a car and an apartment in the university area till Steven, Ellen, our dog Stella and I could join him after a month of being apart. His first day of work he left the motor running on his rented car and locked the keys inside. A secretary told him about his car. Stu told her that he'd left the motor running on purpose because he wanted to get an early start for lunch. It took a while for them to get used to his strange sense of humor as well as his penchant for locking his keys in the car.

He called me one Saturday and said it was 95 degrees in Knoxville that day and he had just come back from playing five sets of tennis with Hal Ernest, one of the account executives at Lavidge & Associates. Hal didn't seem to notice the heat; he had lost every match and wouldn't quit. Stu thinks it's bad manners to quit when you're winning. Hal finally said he'd had enough. Stu, completely dehydrated, was climbing the stairs to his second-floor apartment when both his legs cramped and he had to crawl up the steps on his hands and knees. A man coming down asked if he was OK— did he need help? Stu told him he had just won a tennis tournament for paraplegics.

STARTING A NEW LIFE

In the middle of August we drove down to Knoxville, Tennessee, in our un-air-conditioned Ford Fairlane, and settled into our new house. Steven and Ellen started school at the end of the month. We had one car and I had to drive with Stu to work every morning and pick him up in the evening. I hated doing that. In October Stu's parents came to visit us driving a brand new, bright yellow Ford Fairlane. To our amazement, it was their gift to us, and they flew back to Detroit. Stu hated the color and traded it in for an olive-green Maverick.

Stu loved being Creative Director and did the best work of his career. That October his agency swept the Full-Page Newspaper category winning 1st, 2nd, and 3rd place at the Addy Awards, The following month he was made a vice-president.

The announcement was published in *Art Direction*, a national magazine. It was "just a title" Stu said, but he loved it anyway. He was now the Creative Director of two branch offices, one in Chattanooga, and the other in Greensboro, North Carolina. Stu traveled to both offices once a month. He always drove to Chattanooga and usually flew to North Carolina. Stu got airsick, and once sent a telegram to the people at Lavidge. Some of them actually believed that Piedmont Airlines had sent it, congratulating them because their creative director had vomited on the plane to Greensboro.

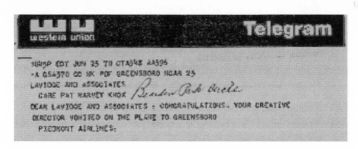

Stu worked on many accounts: Pilot Life Insurance, Roy Rodger's Hamburger Restaurants and Shoney's Big Boy restaurants, Tennessee Hamilton Bank, The Bank of Maryville, and The Heritage Bank of Johnson City, Baptist Children's Hospital, among others. He directed and won awards for a lot of television commercials.

Lavidge acquired the Southern Coffin account in 1971. The client delivered seven coffins to be photographed for an ad in a trade publication. Stu persuaded the photographer to take some photos of him in the coffin—it seemed a lot funnier forty years ago.

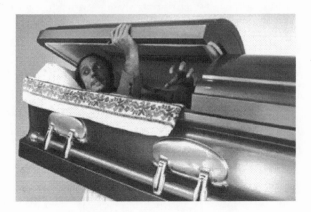

Ellen was then in second grade. When her teacher asked the children in her class to bring a photo of one of their parents to school the following day, Ellen, without asking for permission, brought the photo of her daddy in the coffin. Her teacher was horrified and called me that afternoon. I attempted some kind of apology, but I couldn't stop laughing.

It took me a year to adapt to living in the South. Nobody understood my Brooklyn accent and I could barely understand the East Tennessee twang. After a year of adjusting to our new life, (I'd never been further south than Pennsylvania) I took my portfolio around to all the various ad agencies to try to get some freelance artwork. Most of them said they really liked my work but told me they couldn't use me as long as my husband was with Lavidge & Associates.

One of them, Hogan/Rose, hired me as a freelancer in spite of it and paid me more than any of my other accounts. The University of Tennessee paid me the least, but I loved all the variety in their assignments. I ultimately free-lanced for three years. I thought that Steven and Ellen were still too young to have me working full-time. There was no such thing as day care in 1970, and my mother lived in New York.

AN OLD LOVE

While working at Lavidge and no longer having to commute three hours a day, Stu found he had time to spare and went back to an old love—drawing. He did intricate pencil drawings that took three months to finish and they became so popular that he decided to make limited edition prints of them.

He asked me what I thought about his going into business for himself. I told Stu that he was then forty-one years old and if he didn't try it now, then when could he? He would always wonder what might have happened if he hadn't. He had no idea whether he could support us. Did we really have enough money to pay the mortgage and still continue sending Steven and Ellen to Webb, a private school? I suggested we switch roles.

For the past three years my favorite client was The University of Tennessee. The director of publications often asked me if I'd work for the department fulltime instead of just freelancing. I told Stu if I accepted the job I would only be able to support us in half the style we were accustomed to. My salary would be less than half of his. We decided we'd try. So I accepted the offer from the university and became a graphic designer for the UT Publications Department. I worked there for the next twenty-two years. July 2, 1973, the day I started working at UT, Stu quit his job at Lavidge. He started his own company, and named it "Traditions."

Once a month he traveled around the entire country selling his prints to galleries and a lot of frame shops. He also did many outdoor art shows. During that time he sold 13,000 prints, and we lived just fine. Stu took Steven to his tennis lessons and Ellen to her dancing lessons; he drove in the neighborhood car pool for Webb School; tried to learn how to cook (he couldn't) and shopped for food. He played some tennis every day and could draw whenever he could fit it into his schedule.

Stu never worked for anyone, even himself, for more than five years. In 1978 Stu abandoned "Traditions" and Art Lavidge took him back.

Porch Sittin' A sold out print.

At the age of fifty-nine Stu left advertising for good. Soon after he enrolled at the University of Tennessee as a freshman, majored in Art, and started to paint. He said the worst part was that all the students thought he was the teacher.

Stu has now been a full time painter for more than twenty years. He said if he lived as long as his mother, who died at almost ninety-three, he will have as long a career as a painter as he did in advertising. And he will *always* love his boss.

Stu's painting of a fake wooden cow guarding a barn.

Stu Cooks
(No Photo Available.)

*A perfect waffle is defined as being
crisp and well browned on the outside with a
moist, light, airy and fluffy inside.*

THE MIRACLE OF THE WAFFLE

It was the early morning of November 21, 2010, the second day of a ten-day-car-trip from Saratoga Springs, NY to Stu's family's Thanksgiving reunion in Orlando, Florida. I was sitting at a small table at the Fairfield Inn in North Carolina, eating Honey Nut Cheerios and sliced bananas at their do-it-yourself breakfast, when Stu suddenly appeared beside me holding a paper plate covered in gooey batter. He was totally pissed off.

"This was supposed to be a waffle!" he said, looking baffled.

Stu must have believed in the miracle of the waffle, where, when you pushed down the spigot and batter came out on the paper plate it would somehow turn into a waffle. He never noticed the nearby Waffle Iron. I told him to throw the plate in the garbage and toast a bagel. I laughed *then*, but I didn't laugh almost forty years ago on my first day of working for the university when Stu tried to cook his first dinner.

STU COOKS THE LAST SUPPER

Four years after we moved to Knoxville, Stu quit his job as Vice President of Creative Services at Lavidge & Associates and started his own limited-edition print business. He planned to stay home, draw, and be there for Steven and Ellen when they came home from school. He would also shop for food and cook dinner. He had never done anything in the kitchen before except boil water for tea, but I told him that his planning and cooking the meals was part of the deal. Looking back, I have no idea what I could have been thinking.

I had worked at home as a freelance artist for nearly thirteen years. After my first day of full-time work at the university I was extremely tired. I left the house at eight in the morning and didn't get home until after five in the afternoon. I wasn't used to getting up at 6:00 A.M. and working all day without an afternoon nap. It was a shock to my system, but a bigger shock awaited me at home.

When I opened the door, it smelled as if the house were burning down and someone had used a rubber mat to beat out the flames. I tried to ignore the awful smell, smile, and be a supportive wife. So I said to Stu,

"Hi honey, what did you fix for dinner?"

"Hamburger Helper," he replied.

Far from being a gourmet cook myself, I wouldn't feed 'Hamburger Helper' to anyone, not even to Stella, our dog. I stared at the sink, which was filled to the top with blackened pots and pans. I thought Stu must have burned every cooking utensil we owned. The supportive wife role was heading quickly out the window.

"Isn't 'Hamburger Helper' supposed to be a one-pot meal?" I asked, remembering all the TV commercials.

"That's what it said on the box, but I put all the stuff in a pot and it burned, so I put it in another pot and it burned, and so I put it in another pot and it burned, and . . ." Stu looked mystified. I should have taught him how to work the stove, but for some reason, I thought he knew that there was high heat, medium heat, low heat and all those increments in between.

"You know, Stu, at least you could have cleaned the fucking pots before I got home," I said. The supportive wife bit had gone down the toilet.

"I did," he said, looking abashed. "You should have seen them before."

Now, if you didn't know Stu, you might think he was faking. But Stu can't even work the thermostat. I was always the one who flipped the circuit breakers back and forth in the garage of our Tennessee house when the power went out, even at night in the winter when it was freezing cold. If Stu went out and flipped them, nothing happened. So what could I possibly have been expecting with the stove?

I took full responsibility for the disaster of Stu's first dinner, and we ate out that night. We didn't have any choice. There was only a tiny pile of revolting, burned, chopped meat on a plate. Even if our taste buds were surgically removed, it was hardly enough food for four hungry people. After that I was willing to break our covenant. Stu would continue to do the shopping and the other motherly chores, but I promised to always cook dinner. Since you can't burn lettuce, he would fix the salad.

STU BOILS LUNCH

I was diagnosed with Multiple Sclerosis on May 20th of 1977. It was my fortieth birthday. After my first trip to the hospital in early April, some good things did happen. Our neighbors started bringing food to our house and offering to help in any way they could. News travels fast in small cities like Knoxville and people look out for each other.

By that afternoon, many people in the neighborhood had heard that I had been rushed to the hospital by ambulance in the middle of the night. Many dropped off casseroles, salads, homemade pies and continued to do so for the entire month I was there. The widower across the street brought a prime rib. Stu and the children were eating much better than they ever had before.

I could not even *look* at the hospital food, so Stu brought a fresh cantaloupe from home every day and the nurses would cut it up for me. It was the only thing I ate for the next four weeks. Stu would stay with me for the entire afternoon, go home, have dinner with the children, and then come back later in the evening until visiting hours were over. When I actually got home I could barely walk and I couldn't use my hands at all.

Stu became a nurse that Florence Nightingale would have admired. Every morning he made me tea and toast for breakfast. Every afternoon he boiled a hot dog for my lunch, cut it up in sections and arranged the soft pieces on a plate with some mustard on the side. He bought dinners from restaurants. Three months later, I returned to work and to cooking dinner again.

STU MAKES RESERVATIONS

Once the children were grown and out of the house, we always ate dinner in restaurants. Thinking he could help make our lives easier, Steven sent us a microwave oven. He said we could pop something into it, and in four or five minutes we could have a delicious dinner on the table. I bought ten different microwaveable dinners.

On three different occasions, I popped our dinners in the microwave, put them on the table, took one bite, and said, "I can't eat this shit." Stu didn't seem to mind them, but I think he was faking it. When we still had quite a few dinners left in the freezer and I offered to microwave one, Stu would say, "Fuck it. Let's eat out."

STU CRACKS AN EGG

Eventually, I retired and started cooking dinner for the two of us again. Sometimes I even made breakfast. One morning I was making a healthy salami omelet— Stu's favorite—and I said to him, "You know, before you die, I think you should have the experience of cracking an egg."

"I don't think I can do that," Stu said.

"Sure you can," I counseled. "Now watch what I do carefully. I'll crack the first two and then you'll crack the third one."

This was the detailed lesson I wish I'd given on the use of the stove so many years ago. When Stu cracked the egg and saw the raw yolks staring back at him from the bowl, he said, "That was really disgusting. Please, don't ever ask me to do that again." I never will.

Stu & Oil
Do Not Mix

"MIXING OIL & LEAD"
Stu had an exhibit at the Crandall
Public Library in Glens Falls, NY showing both
Oil Paintings and Pencil Drawings.

Oil and water don't mix.
It's a principle most
seventh-graders know.

Completely out of the blue, on a perfectly ordinary, hot summer evening in Knoxville steam came gushing out from under the hood of my Buick Skyhawk. I had just come home from work, parked in the garage and turned off the engine. The marker on the temperature gauge was past the H.

At that time in our lives, especially now that both children had graduated from college and were no longer living at home, we ate out *every single night*. I always took a nap before we left for dinner. I'd arrive home from work at exactly 5:15 p.m. Stu usually didn't get home until 6:30 or 7:00. By the time we'd left for dinner that night, I had forgotten about the steam coming out from under the hood of my car or that the temperature gauge had gone up past HOT. I didn't remember it until 4:00 in the morning, when I awoke with a start and told Stu that my car had overheated.

Stu was driving to North Carolina on a business trip the next morning and had to leave before dawn. He suggested that we get up and check out my car. As it turned out, we definitely should have stayed in bed.

It took Stu at least half-an-hour to figure out how to open the hood. It was during that lovely era before all the gas stations had switched to self-service; a time when the service station attendant who filled the tank with gas also checked under the hood to make sure the oil and water were at the right level; a time when they actually washed your windshield! It was a time when drivers like us didn't have to *look* under the hoods of our cars—in fact we never even *opened* them.

When Stu finally got the hood open, he pointed to a ridged tank at the front and asked me, "Is that the radiator?"

"I guess so," I said, truly thinking it was. It looked like the radiators that warmed our house when I was a child. Stu screwed off the cap with some difficulty and peered inside. He asked me to bring him a flashlight.

"No wonder your car was steaming," he said with confidence and a touch of scorn. "Your radiator is bone dry! Why don't you bring me a pitcher of water."

I brought out a large pitcher filled with water and Stu poured all of it into the "radiator." He said, rather smugly, that it would take a lot of water to fill it. So I brought out three more pitchers and water suddenly started pouring out all over the floor of the garage. "You must have a leak in your radiator," Stu said knowingly. "You'd better take it to the Buick dealer tomorrow." We both went back to sleep.

Stu woke me up before dawn. "I'm leaving for North Carolina now," he said, bending down to kiss the top of my head. "Don't even *think* of driving your car to the dealer today. I just backed it out of the garage and lots of black smoke gushed out all over the place. Call AAA and have them tow it." The sky was just starting to lighten, and since I was really tired after getting up at 4:00 in the morning, I went back to sleep. Later, when I was dressed, I called AAA.

Within twenty minutes the tow truck arrived. The driver was what people in Tennessee call a "toothless peckerwood," which refers to a stupid-looking man with no teeth. I told the AAA man what had happened. He lifted the hood and asked me to show him exactly where my husband had poured all that water. I immediately pointed to the "radiator." The toothless peckerwood doubled over in laughter.

"Honey, that ain't yer water, that's yer earl," he said, grinning from big ear to big ear. When he was able to stop laughing, he looked me straight in the eye and said rather gleefully, "Ya ruint yer car." I then asked him to please tow my car to the Buick dealer on the Alcoa Highway. He put the gearshift in neutral, jacked up the front, and in less than five minutes he'd put a chain on the Skyhawk's front bumper, attached it to his tow truck and we were on our way. It looked as if my poor little Skyhawk might never fly again.

I sat next to the toothless peckerwood in the cab of his truck. Every half mile or so he'd stop his truck, laugh some more and repeat, "Ya ruint yer car." He drove slowly and carefully to the Buick dealer, stopping only to laugh and tell me once again, that I had ruined my car.

"Don't get out of this truck. Don't say a word," I said to him coldly when we'd arrived at the dealer's. "I want to tell them what happened myself."

He didn't pay me the slightest bit of attention, but jumped out of the cab and sprinted into the shop, undoubtedly to tell the servicemen about the dumb Yankees who had poured gallons of water into their oil tank. He then may have commiserated with them about how in God's name the Union Army had managed to defeat the Confederacy. The outcome of the Civil War was still being debated in the south.

"Did my husband really ruin my car?" I asked the repairman, who actually managed to keep a straight face. "Maybe, maybe not," he quietly told me. "We'll flush the tank out a few times and put in new oil. Hopefully we can save it." Saving our 1982 Buick cost $650.00. It was probably more than a twelve-year-old Skyhawk was worth.

In 1994 the Skyhawk's air-conditioner died. I could not drive a car in the Tennessee heat without air-conditioning, so I sold the car to a friend for $400.

Since her son had just gotten his learner's permit, she gave the Skyhawk to him for his 16th birthday. It made me happy that the hawk would fly once more — hopefully not too fast. I used the $400 as the down payment on a brand new, tough little Saturn.

My new Saturn would survive many traumas in its twelve years of living with us. A truck sideswiped it in the second week we owned it. A few years later, the door and fender were crushed after an accident on the Alcoa Highway Bridge. Ten years later, Stu left that spunky little Saturn sinking in quicksand while he did an oil painting of an abandoned car with a crushed hood and a missing engine that was sitting behind a puddle, surrounded by weeds and mud. It looked like the car version of a toothless peckerwood.

Stu, Stella, Midnight & Me

Stu and I stand in front of the Tennessee
house we shared with Stella, our dog
and Midnight, our cat.

It is an age-old dilemma:
How do you get a fastidious feline and
a curious canine to live in harmony? After all,
there's a reason people use the expression
"fighting like cats and dogs."

After our children were born, Stu and I fought like
cats and dogs over whether or not to get a dog. I kept
insisting that every child should have a dog. I'd always
wanted a dog of my own, but my mother wouldn't let
me, I told him looking for understanding and sympathy.
Steven, at that time, was seven-years-old and Ellen was
four. So two years after we moved into our first house,
Stu finally decided he didn't want to fight anymore.

One day, without saying a word to me, he went to a
pet shop by himself and fell in love with a Chinese pug
puppy. He took me there right away, before anyone else
could buy her. I also fell in love—she was tiny and so
ugly that she was beautiful. We named her Stella after
the wife of Stanley Kowalski in *A Streetcar Named
Desire*. Stu wanted to go outside in a torn T-shirt and,
like Stanley Kowalski, yell "Stell-aaahh."

The only time Stella was ever frisky was in the pet
shop that sold her to us. The first night we had her, she
whimpered all night and Steven took his blanket
downstairs and slept on the couch to keep the scared
puppy company. The following day we took Stella to a
veterinarian for a check-up.

The vet told us the dog was sickly and we should
take it back to the pet store. Of course Stella had
already spent a night with us. Stu once refused to
return a damaged *lamp* that had spent a night in our
house. He would never return a *living creature* that had
spent the night.

THE NOVELTY WEARS OFF

The novelty of having a dog wore off when the children realized that the only thing Stella wanted to do was sit on her blanket and chew on her rawhide bone. She had zero interest in frolicking outside with them, and eventually they hardly noticed that we had a dog.

So Stella became solely my responsibility. I was the one who fed her, took her for walks, drove her to the vet and grew to love her. Our house was not air-conditioned and Stella, with her pushed-in-face, had trouble breathing in the summer. Stu said we could call in a specialist from Germany to help Stella breathe. I suggested installing central air-conditioning. We *all* breathed a lot easier after we air-conditioned the house.

STELLA LOVES TO EAT

When Stella was a puppy, the vet advised me to cook a scrambled egg for her every morning. I did this until our puppy became so fat that I had to put her on RD (Reducing Diet.) A Pug is a chowhound and will eat everything in sight. Poor little Stella wolfed down her food so quickly that she would sometimes choke. Stella gagging on her food occasionally required me to perform the Heimlich maneuver, but giving our dog mouth-to-mouth-resuscitation was out of the question.

Stella was forever sick with *something* and she was always on a special diet. She was eventually put on ID (Intestinal Diet) and KD (Kidney Diet.) She had zillions of allergies—the vet frequently prescribed Prednisone for her. The disgusting (to me) smell of her special-diet-canned-food made me want to gag, but every morning I cut it into small chunks and gave her only a little bit at a time so that I could, with any luck, avoid performing the Heimlich maneuver. However, since I was the one who insisted we get a dog I couldn't really complain. The upside was that as soon as anyone dropped a piece of food, Stella was on it in a flash, so our kitchen and dining room floors were always spotless.

After puppy-hood, Stella did nothing but sit on her shaggy-rug-blanket and nibble away on her chewy-bone. Whenever she changed location, she held the blanket between her teeth and dragged it everywhere she went. When chewing on her rawhide bone she appeared to be smoking a cigar. Stella actually bore quite a startling resemblance to Winston Churchill. Ellen once said she thought her stuffed frog was more fun than that dog.

In early August of 1969, our family moved from New York to Tennessee. Stella was two years old. She rode in the back of the car with Steven and Ellen. Since our Ford Fairlane didn't yet have air-conditioning, they fed Stella chunks of ice to help her stay cool.

STELLA MEETS MIDNIGHT

Two weeks after we moved to Knoxville a black cat showed up at our front door. I wondered if it was an omen, but I gave it all the leftover macaroni and cheese from our dinner. Stu hated cats because his mother did. She'd often told her children horrible stories about cats attacking children in cribs. Stu told me to get rid of the cat, or at least not to feed it.

But I had already fed the stray and it wasn't going away. She was about six-months old—pure black with yellow eyes. I named her Midnight. I told Stu that Midnight was now my cat. He said if I wanted to keep it outside I could, but there was no way that cat was ever coming in the house. On a cold December day, I called Stu at work and told him that Midnight was standing at the front door and she was sneezing.

"Well, don't leave her out there. Bring her in," he said. It turned out he had been playing with Midnight every morning before he went to work and had decided he didn't detest cats after all.

Stella and Midnight hit it off right from the start. They chased each other around the house—just playing. They didn't fight. It was more exercise than Stella had gotten in quite a while. She didn't like to go for walks anymore. The day after a snowstorm hit Huntington Station, I had taken her for her daily walk. Salt, that the highway department put on the street. must have burned her feet. From that day on she wouldn't walk *away* from the house. To take Stella for a walk I had to carry her for about a half-mile. Then, as soon as I put her on the ground, she walked straight home.

STU GOES TO THE VET

Carlos Webb, DVM, was a good veterinarian and a nice man, but his receptionist was a virtual moron. Stu quickly picked up on the fact that she believed any stupid thing he told her. When he brought Stella in for her frequent visits, he used to tell the receptionist that Stella would no longer answer to her name, so we were changing it to: Georgette, Violetta, Camellia, Estelle, or whatever new name popped into his head. She always took Stella's records out of the file cabinet, crossed out the old name and wrote in the new one. Stu eventually tired of thinking up new names and changed our dog's name back to Stella.

Stu once told Dr. Webb's receptionist that I was now eating Stella's food and he wondered if it would make me sick. (The smell of our dog's food did make me want to throw up in the morning.) He told her I just *loved* the taste. Before he could stop her, the receptionist swiftly ran to another room and brought Dr. Webb back with her to answer Stu's question.

At that point Stu had to pretend he was serious. Dr. Webb surely knew he was kidding. "It won't make her sick, but it may make her fat," he said with a perfectly straight face. But perhaps the most outrageous story Stu told the receptionist was that we wanted to teach Stella to kill and asked her if she could recommend a place where our dog could be trained. "Well, there isn't anyplace in Knoxville that I know of, but you might try Johnson City," she advised.

MIDNIGHT

Midnight was very smart, but poor Stella stayed an innocent forever. When she left her blanket unoccupied to get a drink of water or something, Midnight would lie down on it like a sleeping child. When Stella came back to reclaim her only lifelong possession, Midnight would hiss at her. Stella would stand there mystified, never understanding the betrayal.

Midnight often behaved like a naughty child. Every night we used to let our cat go outside to hunt. Whenever she'd had enough of killing small creatures, she would jump on the outside sill of our bedroom window and pull on the screen with her claws until one of us got out of bed and let her in.

So we locked her in the bathroom at night. When she knew it was about lockup time she'd hide under our bed—right in the center so we couldn't reach her with our hands. Each and every night we had to swing the baseball bat under the bed to chase her out. When we'd first put her in the bathroom, she'd pluck at the doorstop continually, until we finally screwed it into the *top* of the door.

When one of her family was sick, however, Midnight would sit, with or on them, until they felt better. When, in 1977, I had to spend three months at home after being diagnosed with Multiple Scleroses she hardly left my side. When I lay down on the couch she would sit on me, purring, as if to cheer me up. We called her "nurse pussycat."

Nurse pussycat caring for her patient.

STELLA'S DECLINE

Two weeks after Ellen's fourteenth birthday Steven left for a year in France. He had been chosen by the American Field Service to be an exchange student. He was Ellen's best friend and she missed him terribly.

The entire house suffered in one way or another from Steven's absence—even Stella, who had taken to peeing on Ellen's carpeting every day. Stu eventually had to put up a cardboard barrier so that the little Pug couldn't get in. Ellen wrote in large letters on the cardboard: NO TRESSPISSING. She wrote in a letter to her brother:

HOW STELLA ALMOST BECAME A HAND PUPPET: Well, one night Mommy was reading a magazine that said one cause for multiple sclerosis is having a small, sickly, housedog for over ten years. Since Stella's tenth birthday is today, we were discussing that for my safety, and Stella's misery of life anyway, that we should . . . we should . . . put . . . Stella . . . to sleep. (Would she even know the difference?)

After dinner I said to Dad, "Yuck, did you know that when the vet puts a dog to sleep he gives you the dog's body afterward?" And Dad seriously replied, "Actually, I think they just give you the skin . . . you know . . . so you can take it home . . . you can even make a hand-puppet out of it . . . so you don't miss the dog!!!" Isn't that disgusting?

It was Stella's peeing everywhere that finally did it. We had Dr. Webb put her to sleep—she was thirteen—ninety-one in dog years. When I got home from work that day, Stu was sitting at the kitchen table staring straight ahead; he couldn't seem to speak. He had just come back from the vet's. Stu's eyes still fill with tears when he thinks about it. I truly felt nothing but relief.

EPILOGUE: DUSK

One day there was a gray cat sitting on our porch. I invited her in, but as soon as Midnight saw her, they began fighting. They hated each other on sight. I put Midnight outside to sulk and gave the gray cat some evaporated milk. I named her Dusk.

In spite of the fact that Dusk continued to hate Midnight, she decided she would really like to live with that nice family who was feeding her. This started what I called, "The Rotating Pussycat System." When Dusk arrived, Midnight went outside for a while. Midnight always slept in the bathroom, while Dusk, who was either a night owl or just trying to kill one, *never* slept in the house. Dusk didn't ever show affection for any of us. She never sat on our laps and purred like Midnight.

On a hot August morning, I went outside and Dusk was lying on her back, gasping for breath. I rushed her to Dr. Webb's office. He took one look at her and told me she was going to die. I broke into tears. The following day his receptionist called to tell me that Dusk had miraculously recovered and I could pick her up. They gave me some medicine for her. This scenario replayed several more times.

One afternoon, Stu and I were driving home when we saw what appeared to be a gray lump on the road behind our house. A car had obviously hit Dusk. Her eye was out of its socket and her jaw was broken. I told Stu to get a blanket from the house. While I stood in the street screaming, I seemed to be watching myself from a place outside of my body.

I wrapped Dusk in the blanket and held her on my lap while she looked straight at me with her one good eye. Stu then drove to Dr. Webb's office, but his clinic was closed for two weeks while he was on vacation. He had left a note with an in-case-of-emergency address and phone number on his front door. Stu then drove to the emergency veterinarian's office, which was several miles away.

It was the year when ex-president Harry Truman was gravely ill and on life support. I used to say, "Why don't they just let the poor man die?" When the emergency vet asked, "Do you want me to put her to sleep or try to save her?" I said, to my own amazement, "Try to save her." A few hours later, he called and told me she had died. He asked me if I wanted to pick up her body and bury her. I told him I didn't. I cried for the rest of the day. I just realized while writing this, that after two years of living with us, we didn't have a single photo of Dusk. We lost Midnight to cancer nine years later.

MOVING AWAY

When we decided to leave Knoxville and move to Saratoga Springs, Stu asked me if I wanted to get a dog or maybe a cat.

"You've got to be kidding," I said. "I never want to be responsible for another living thing as long as I live— and I'm not too sure about *you*."

Now, if a yellow cat showed up at my door I would not feed it and name it Noon. If a white cat appeared I would not feed it and name it Dawn. I lived my first eighteen years without Stu and, so far, the next fifty-six years with him. I still love *him*, but I'm not sure I even *like* dogs and cats anymore.

Stu Goes on Vacation

Stu enjoys the slide at the
Ontario, Canada Welcome Center.

*Columbus believed that he had
found the Indies. He hadn't.
He got lost, but claimed it for Spain nevertheless.
The crew saw sandpipers, native to the
Americas, for the first time.*

Jack O'Brien, Elford Alley

Left: Stu claims an island off the coast of South Carolina.
Right: Stu tries to befriend a native bird. He had persuaded
a native of Brooklyn to take the photos.

Like Christopher Columbus, Stu loves to travel, but
frequently he also gets lost. It seems clear that neither
one of them had much of a sense of direction. In early
October of 1492, Columbus faced a mutiny because the
crew thought they were lost in the middle of the ocean.
He was barely able to stop the first rebellion, but three
days later there was a second mutiny by his crew. The
sailors wanted to throw Columbus overboard. He had to
promise to return to Spain if they did not find land in
three more days. Two days later, they finally reached
the New World. Going on a vacation with Stu also has
its stresses. I sympathized with the mutineers.

A VACATION WITH STU IS NO PICNIC

The first "real" vacation we took was in 1959, three
days after we graduated from Pratt Institute. We'd had
to fit our honeymoon into four days during Pratt's 1956
Christmas break, and we worked every summer for the
rest of our student years.

On June 8, 1959, Stu's twenty-seventh birthday, we
took off for a summer in Europe. We'd decided to spend
the $5,000 that my great-uncle, Alexander Friedman,
had left me in his will on a few months of carefree
travel. We had no jobs. We didn't have children. We
were living in my parents' basement apartment. We had
no responsibilities at all.

Stu wanted to fly because of the awful experiences he'd had both going to and coming home from the Korean War. I'd wanted to take a slow boat because I didn't want to wake up in Europe three days after graduation. I needed some time to adjust. Knowing zero about ships, I assured Stu that a luxury liner was different from a troop transport. I, who grew up three miles from Coney Island, was never sick on anything that turned you upside down, or whipped you around in a circle. Stu couldn't watch the merry-go-round without feeling nauseated. We compromised by agreeing to take a ship to Holland and then fly home from Ireland. He took Dramamine. I didn't. I started throwing up before we'd passed the Statue of Liberty.

The ocean liner was nothing like the rides in Coney Island. The ship looked like a big hotel, but it rocked, ever so gently, and I couldn't get off it for nine more days. Justifiably getting even, Stu sent everyone back home postcards with cartoons he drew of me puking over the rail. He wrote, "This is a picture of Greta, on our way to Europe, poisoning the fish." We had crossed the Atlantic on Holland America Lines and docked in Amsterdam. I was never so happy in my entire life to put my feet on solid ground.

Our first day in Amsterdam we checked into a small hotel in one of the neighborhoods listed in the tourist book, "Europe on $5.00 a Day." We spent the rest of the day walking along the 17th century canals. I took a lot of pictures of Stu in his new wooden shoes, etc. After we came home and saw them developed we found that all of our photos had come out a light greenish color. Before leaving for Europe we had bought twenty-five rolls of outdated film. All of the 8 mm movies we took came out just fine.

I hadn't been *anywhere* before and my excitement was overwhelming. It was also exhausting and by 9:30 that night I was ready for bed. Stu seemed to think I was just going to rest for a while and at 10:00 he asked me where I wanted to go for dinner. I told him if he thought I was going out again, I would be heading for the airport and flying home. I again sympathized with the mutineers on the *Santa Maria*.

TILTING AT WINDMILLS

Stu agreed we could wait until breakfast to go out again. We spent the next day visiting windmills and tulip fields and took zillions of pictures with our new camera. We had bought the outdated film from the photo shop that had sold us the Yashica Mat, plus the movie camera, and all the film for both.

After we came home from our trip, the owner of the shop said he felt terrible that none of the photos we took came out, so he would give us a free screen on which we could watch our movies. He did not offer to send us back to Europe.

POSTCARD FROM THE CAVE

Stu and I visited one of the many caves in northern Spain from a Stone Age culture that lasted from around 20,000 BC to the end of the last Ice Age in about 8000 BC. The oldest pieces of human bone in Europe have been found in Spain; they probably came from ancestors of the later Neanderthals. A piece of bone is thought to be from the skull of an infant ancestor of Homosapiens, who was most likely eaten by a giant hyena more than a million years ago. Stu sent my parents a postcard with a photo of the inside of the huge cave.

Dear Hedda and John,

Greta and I saw the most amazing underground caverns in Spain. It was only about 50 degrees down there and it was good to get out of the heat for a while. It has been the hottest summer in Europe in more than 100 years.

Greta must have wandered off from the group because when we all finally came out she wasn't with us. The tour guide said we couldn't go back inside at this late hour, but she'll probably turn up when it opens again in the morning.

Love,
Stu

I'm sure my mother thought a hyena had eaten me. My father, however, always got the joke. We traveled around Europe for three months and I took lots of photos: Stu holding up the Leaning Tower of Pisa; Stu checking his watch against the time on Big Ben; Stu posing like a gargoyle next to one of the many on Notre Dame Cathedral, etc. "Greta from Brooklyn" was now a world traveler.

We swore we would return, by air of course, every five years. Thirty years later we did. We traveled to the former Soviet Union, but none of our pictures came out there, either. The X-Rays, that everyone's luggage was subjected to before boarding Aeroflot, must have zapped the film. This was twelve years before 9/11. Now all the airlines zap your body as well as your luggage. I wonder if we were simply not meant to take still pictures on the other side of the Atlantic.

We came home in early September and got jobs right away; two weeks later I found out that was pregnant. Three years later, when our daughter was three months old, we left her with a baby-nurse and drove to Quebec, Canada. We thought Steven would like having us all to himself for a while.

A THREE-WEEK VACATION

Stu called me one Friday afternoon in July of 1967 and told me to pack our bags. Gardner Advertising had just told him he could take three weeks off because he'd been working so much overtime without extra pay for the past few months and was doing such a great job. (They fired him the following year.)

The next day we were on our way to the Canadian Rockies in our 1960 Plymouth Valiant, spending a week first in Yellowstone Park and ultimately driving 7,000 miles before returning to Huntington Station. We had to cross a thousand miles of the flat Midwestern plains to get to our destination.

For seven-year-old Steven and four-year-old Ellen, sitting in the back of our un-air-conditioned car must have been a form of torture. They argued constantly for most of their virtual imprisonment.

"Look at the beautiful mountains," I said when we drove through the Rockies.

"It's just a bunch of rocks," they answered in unison.

Steven and Ellen are miserable in the Badlands of South Dakota.

The view from the window improved markedly for Steven and Ellen as we were driving on a narrow road behind a Winnebago. A boy was mooning us from the little window in the back of the van, where his parents probably sent him because he kept complaining about how bored he was with the view of the Rockies. I wondered what that kid would write on his "What I Did On My Summer Vacation" paper in September.

We finally arrived at Yellowstone Park and tried to check into the Old Faithful Inn. They said there was no room at the Inn. "You know what happened the last time they wouldn't let Jews stay at the Inn?" Stu asked. The desk clerk didn't tell us to go to the manger, but did find a room for us at another nearby hotel. As soon as we dropped off our luggage we headed out to see Old Faithful's geyser erupt in its hourly date with mobs of tourists.

Steven was thrilled. The geysers, otherworldly rock formations, the steaming earth impressed even Ellen and she stopped looking unhappy for a little while. In the Canadian Rockies we took a "snow-cat" ride over the Athabasca Glacier—a legacy of the ice age—and looked down a blue crevasse that was one thousand feet deep. Stu wanted to drive to Alaska, but I refused. It would have added another 2,000 miles to our trip. 7,000 miles was as much fun as the children and I could manage. Another three-week vacation would not happen again until we retired.

DIFFERENT VIEWS OF THE GRAND CANYON

By June 5, 1985, Ellen had graduated from college and Steven from Law School. Stu and I wanted to see the Grand Canyon before that United States Senator, whose name I no longer remember, pushed through his plan for erecting another dam on the Colorado River so Las Vegas could get some more water. That great river's rushing water actually created the Grand Canyon.

Stu climbs out of the Grand Canyon

The only way we could reach our destination, other than driving 4,000 miles across the country and then back on a two-week vacation was flying on Delta Air to Las Vegas and then taking Air Nevada to the Grand Canyon. We spent our first night in Las Vegas and the following day, rushed to the airport for an early-morning flight. We didn't have time for breakfast, but there was a shop at the airport that sold milkshakes for

$4.00 each, which twenty-five years ago was pretty expensive.

We ordered two chocolate shakes. I took one sip and said to Stu, "I just can't drink this. It tastes like liquid plastic." I bought a delicious $4.00 cookie instead. Stu thought the shake tasted fine (he liked army food). He stopped me just before I threw my shake in the garbage can and he drank the rest of it. A big mistake.

Air Nevada turned out to be a tiny plane that seated ten people according to their weight. Stu sat in the left front and I sat in the back right. When flying low over the painted-desert I sat next to a bald man who, when the flight became turbulent, hit his head several times on the air vent over the seat, bleeding quite a bit. I sat with my face pressed against the window. Unlike the ship crossing the Atlantic Ocean, this felt more like the rides in Coney Island that I knew and loved.

I shortly heard the sound of "Two-Milkshake-Stu" throwing up. Everyone on the plane eventually had to pass his or her vomit bag to him. During the half-hour flight, he filled them all. A van from the hotel we were staying at picked us up at the tiny airport. Stu's face was green, but that didn't stop the Native-American driver of the van from telling us about the great food at the hotel. Stu had to ask him to stop the van twice so he could get out and throw up.

Stu recovered quickly and that afternoon we took a bus to the canyon. The Grand Canyon is eighteen miles wide in some places, a mile deep, and a stunning sight to see. We heard some kid whine: "It's just a big hole in the ground," and sympathized with his parents. We wanted to walk the trail to the bottom of the canyon, but heard it was always more than ninety degrees down there. We also heard from some people upon returning, that you have to step in, or over, piles of mule shit along the way.

BIKING WITH STEVEN

In October 1994 Steven met us on Nantucket Island off the coast of Massachusetts. On our first day there we went to the beach, a short walk from our motel. The following day we rented ten-speed bikes for a sixteen-mile trip around the hilly island. I hadn't been on a bike in thirty-five years. I had never used a shift before but it was great and I loved it. But I had never before sat on a hard, skinny seat (other than my own) for more than several hours. After biking ten miles to the middle of nowhere, I thought my butt would break. So I said to Steven: "Get on your little yuppie phone and call a cab because I'm not getting back on that bike."

The cab arrived and the driver loaded the bike into the trunk and drove me back to the hotel. Stu and Steven finished the sixteen miles, even though Stu later told me that his ass was *killing* him. Neither Stu nor Steven is quick to quit anything once they have started.

Left: Steven and me enjoying the beach.
Right: Stu and me before I refused to get back on the bike.

STU GETS LOST

For the Thanksgiving reunion of Stu's family in 2010, we planned to drive from Saratoga Springs, New York to Orlando, Florida. We hadn't taken a *really* long car trip in quite a few years and weren't sure our old bodies could survive it. Ever since our traumatic flight from San Francisco to Chicago in 1986 where we sat on the tarmac for almost twelve hours along with 250 other prisoners of American Airlines, we refused to fly again.

We had made reservations at the Homewood Suites in Orlando where Stu's entire family was staying. We'd been on the road for five days and arrived at the hotel at 2:30 on Wednesday afternoon. There was going to be a big party at 7:00 to celebrate Stu's brother Marvin and Marilyn's fiftieth wedding anniversary. We had more than enough time, so Stu went out to run at 3:00 while I rested. He should have been taking a hot shower by 5:45, but by 6:30 he still wasn't back. Now it was pitch dark and I thought a car might have hit him. I called the front desk and told the clerk Stu was missing.

She called me at 6:45 and said a police car had just brought him back. Stu had made a wrong turn and then forgot which hotel we were staying at. He thought if he just kept running, the hotel would appear—the way the New World did for Columbus two days after the crew had threatened mutiny.

Stu hadn't planned on running a marathon that day, so eventually he stopped at a Holiday Inn and told the woman at the front desk that he couldn't remember where he was staying. There are a lot of old people in South Florida, and I'm sure some of them had wandered off and that Stu wasn't the first and wouldn't be the last to forget where he was. But I'll bet the other old people hadn't run ten miles before somebody helped them find where they were going.

At the Holiday Inn where Stu went for help, there was a long line waiting to check in for the Thanksgiving holiday. Even so, the desk clerk called every hotel in the area to see if "a Stu Eichel" was registered there. After phoning about thirty hotels without success, she called the police; she still kept phoning more hotels to find out where the lost runner was staying.

The very next place she called was *our* Homewood Suites. The police officer arrived and asked Stu if he'd like a ride back to his hotel. Stu's brother Marvin had pulled up at the front door of the Homewood Suites at the exact time the policeman brought his older brother back.

"This is the last time you're ever going to see me," Stu told Marvin, "because when I get back to the room Greta is going to kill me."

IF I'M FOUND . . .

The Saratoga Stryders, the group that Stu runs with every Saturday morning, once suggested that everyone buy an ID bracelet, since most runners don't carry any identification. Stu never wore it. After coming home from Florida, he found the ID bracelet tucked away in a dresser drawer. He was grateful he wasn't wearing it the night he got lost in Orlando.

The bracelet gave Stu's name, address, and phone number. For instructions he wrote: Please push body to side of road.

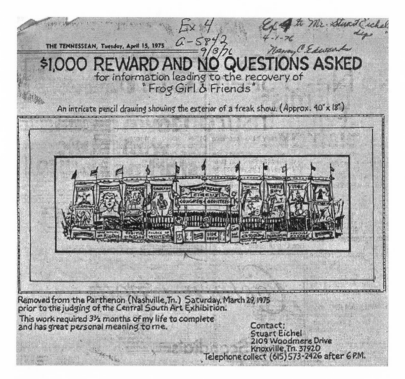

THE TENNESSEAN, Tuesday, April 15, 1975

$1,000 REWARD AND NO QUESTIONS ASKED
for information leading to the recovery of
"Frog Girl & Friends"

An intricate pencil drawing showing the exterior of a freak show. (Approx. 40" x 18")

Removed from the Parthenon (Nashville, Tn.) Saturday, March 29, 1975
prior to the judging of the Central South Art Exhibition.

This work required 3½ months of my life to complete
and has great personal meaning to me.

Contact:
Stuart Eichel
2109 Woodmere Drive
Knoxville, Tn. 37920
Telephone collect (615) 573-2426 after 6 P.M.

Stu's Stolen Drawing

The Tennessean newspaper published a
story about the theft of Stu's drawing,
"Frog Girl & Friends," from The Parthenon
Museum in Nashville.

Freak shows were much more popular
fifty years ago than they are today.
More often than not, the customers would
be extremely disappointed, because most
of these shows were a sham.

Shell Harris

Monsters had always both fascinated and terrified Stu. He saw every horror movie that came to Detroit and then had terrible nightmares afterwards. In the 1940s, when he was about ten years old, his parents' restaurant was directly across the street from the Michigan State Fairgrounds. The main attraction for Stu was the freak show. By the time he was thirteen he had saved enough of his allowance to see it. He was stunned and disappointed to find only a bunch of pitiful, disfigured people. Even now, he can picture the "8 Foot Man" sitting on a chair, totally bored, answering onlookers' dumb questions.

GOING TO THE FAIR

After moving to Knoxville in 1969, we never missed the Tennessee Valley State Fair. Stu loved going after dark when it was all lit up. The day after we attended, in 1974, Stu went back to the fair at noon and took about 100 Polaroid photos of the outside of the Side Show. He would never go "inside" again.

Stu spent the next six months creating "Frog Girl & Friends," the largest and most time-consuming pencil drawing he'd ever done. The highly detailed drawing showed a long line of tents, flags, and ten huge posters depicting the strange, the amazing, the unbelievable people inside—Alive & in Person! The barker in the drawing stands calmly, for the moment, his hands resting on the podium. A painted clock is set at 2:00, its big hands moved hourly, by hand, to the next starting time. At exactly 2:00 o'clock the barker would throw out his arms and shout: "Step right up folks to the Super Circus sideshow. You absolutely won't believe your eyes." The sign promises: "Oddities on Parade." In less politically correct times we called it "The Freak Show."

An artist friend drove to Nashville to deliver Stu's artwork, along with his own, for the judging of the Central South Exhibition at the Parthenon. Stu would pick them up when the show was over. The judging would take place on April 1st and 2nd. On March 30th Stu brought the framed drawing to the UT Publications Department, so that my fellow-artists and the editors could see it. That was the last time anyone *we* knew saw "Frog Girl & Friends."

THE FROG GIRL IS MISSING

The sign at the entrance to the Parthenon Museum stated in bold type: "We do not allow food, drinks, gum, pets, backpacks or oversized bags in the building." With so many rules in place and the guards to enforce them, it's a wonder how, on March 29, 1975, art thieves were able to walk out of the building with Stu's 40"x18" framed drawing as well as the paintings of two other artists.

Whoever stole the artworks knew what they were doing. All three of the artists whose work was stolen had won awards the previous year at the Parthenon's annual Central South Exhibition. One of the stolen works was by a man from Alabama who had won Best of Show for his large oil painting; Stu had won First Place in the drawing category; and the third work was a watercolor that had won First Place.

For the past three years Stu had submitted work for the prestigious exhibit and had always won an award. Surprisingly this time he received a postcard stating his drawing had been rejected. He drove the two hundred miles to Nashville to pick it up and when he got there was informed that his drawing was "missing." Stu told me that for a split second he was happy it hadn't been rejected after all. A Parthenon official said they were still trying to find the missing work. She told Stu that the Parthenon hadn't notified the three artists earlier, because they didn't want to alarm them.

When Stu called her a few days later, she told him his drawing, as well as the work of the other two other artists, had also been stolen. A representative from the Parthenon had called the police to report the theft. The three artists were invited to a meeting with a detective from the Nashville Police Department.

THE DETECTIVE

Stu and I drove to Nashville, but he was the only artist to show up. Representatives of the Parthenon and the Tennessee Art League, co-sponsors of the exhibit, pointed out that Stu had signed a release stating: "Due care will be taken, but the Parthenon and the Tennessee Art League are not responsible for anything lost, stolen or damaged." Stu had signed many such releases before, so this was not unusual.

The detective, who looked like he was right out of central casting, asked questions for which there were no satisfactory answers. It turned out that "due care" had *not* been taken. All the floors of the downstairs galleries were covered with 843 pieces of art, lying face-up for judging. Guards were supposed to be monitoring the huge rooms but had left their posts before the judging even began. It was revealed later that the guards *always* left their posts to sell souvenirs in the gift shop whenever a busload of tourists arrived.

Mrs. Evans from the Parthenon told the detective that the Tennessee Art League, and *not* the Parthenon, sponsored the Central South Exhibition. Mrs. Jones, first vice-president of the league, said the Parthenon was co-sponsoring the event with her organization. Mrs.

Evans said she understood all the pieces of art for the Central South show were the responsibility of the league until they are placed on the walls for viewing. "We have at least a million people come through here every year and we haven't had any trouble before," Mrs. Evans said.

The Art League representative disagreed. She had heard that artwork had been stolen directly off the walls where they were being exhibited and said that Mrs. Evans had told someone it would be impossible to have a guard at the shows because park police already have "too much to do." Mrs. Evans quickly broke in and said, "I did not tell her that. Someone else may have."

Mrs. Jones told the detective she understood the Parthenon always provided security at art shows. She said the art league members were busy working with 843 pieces of art in two rooms and two hallways at the Parthenon. "I feel dreadful about this," she said.

The detective gave everyone his card and asked us to call him if we had new information.

Before leaving for Nashville, Stu had done a hasty sketch of his drawing and created a poster that offered:

"$1,000 Reward and <u>NO</u> Questions Asked for Information Leading to the Recovery of "Frog Girl & Friends"

After the meeting we drove to *The Tennessean*, the #1 newspaper in Nashville and we showed the poster to them. They asked Stu if they could have it and the next day published a front-page story about the theft.

THE PSYCHIC

Stu called me at work a few days after our return from Nashville and asked if I could come home right away. He said if what just happened was true, we'd never be the same again. When I arrived he was standing in the driveway waiting for me. He had called his twin brother in New York to tell him about the theft and Edward had given him the phone number of a psychic in North Carolina who was famous as "a finder of lost objects." Stu thought it was ridiculous, but called the psychic anyway. The only thing he told him was, "I'm Stu Eichel. I just had a drawing stolen from the Parthenon in Nashville."

"I see who took it," the psychic said immediately.

He "saw" two young women who had stolen it for their "boyfriend," an artist, who was going to use the drawing as a model to paint from and then destroy it. He even described what the women were wearing and, in detail, the house where the artist lived.

Stu then called the detective from Nashville, who had given him his card, "I feel like an idiot," he said, "but I just spoke to a psychic . . . "

The detective interrupted him: "Don't feel like an idiot. We deal with them all the time. We just don't publicize it." So Stu repeated the psychic's description of the two women and the house where their artist friend lived.

"I know the residence," the detective said. "It's an unusual house. I'm going over there right now to check it out." He called Stu about two hours later and told him he'd been to the house. An artist *had* lived there, but he'd recently moved, leaving no forwarding address.

Stu immediately thought of the poster he'd done that had appeared on the front page of *The Tennessean*, showing the drawing and offering a reward. We would have hired a private detective to see if he could find the man, but we didn't have the money; in fact, if someone had claimed the $1,000 reward, we would have had to get a loan from the bank. There are a lot of murders in Nashville. We realized that the Nashville police weren't about to devote more manpower to a stolen drawing.

YOU CAN BEAT CITY HALL

Stu was devastated by the loss. He then decided to sue the City of Nashville. Even though he had signed a release, he felt "due care" had not been taken. The unguarded work had been stolen before the judging had even started.

Stu phoned the artist in Birmingham, and asked if he wanted to join him in a lawsuit against the City of

Nashville. "I can't right now," he said. "My girlfriend recently attacked me with a knife and drove my car into the river."

Stu talked to a lawyer in Knoxville, who then spoke to an attorney in Nashville, who agreed to take the case on a contingency basis. Several weeks later we met with the Nashville lawyer in his office. The next time we saw him was more than a year later in the City of Nashville Courthouse. I sat on a hard wooden bench outside the courtroom for at least three hours. As a witness, I was not allowed to hear anything that was said before my testimony.

After I was excused, I was allowed to remain in the courtroom and listen to the last person testify. I overheard Stu say to his lawyer when Mrs. Jones from the art league testified, "She's lying." His lawyer had whispered, "Everyone lies in court." That was news to us. The woman from the Tennessee Art League had told Stu an entirely different story when she'd spoken to him. Stu thought she must have been under a lot of pressure from other members of the league not to take *any* responsibility for the stolen artwork.

Su was awarded $7,000 by the judge: the lawyer's percentage was $3,000. The $4.000 that remained was hardly compensation for six months of work, but it was a victory of sorts. Both the City of Nashville and the Tennessee Art League were required to split the cost. Art League members were assessed $10 each towards settlement of the claim. Some of them were furious at Stu. Sometime later, he ran into a woman he knew, who was a member of the League. She snarled at him and said, "You're a cockroach." The leading southern art magazine, *Sunshine Artist*, had branded any artist who tried to harm another artist "a cockroach."

However, another artist congratulated Stu for beating city hall. "The Parthenon never took care of the artwork," he said. "After an exhibition, they left my paintings in a damp moldy cellar. I'll bet they'll be more careful from now on," he added.

BLOCKHEAD & FRIENDS

Stu couldn't bear to look at his Polaroid photos of
the fair for seven more years. Then, in 1983 he finished
a smaller version of the midway—showing three of the
nine posters. When the prints of "Blockhead & Friends"
were released, stories appeared in *The Knoxville News-
Sentinel* and *The Knoxville Journal*.

EPILOGUE

By the summer of 1996, more than twenty years after the loss of Frog Girl & Friends, Stu had been a full-time painter for the past five years and I had retired from the University of Tennessee. To get away from the heat, we rented a house way up north in Saratoga Springs, New York. We fell in love with the area and in 2000 we sold our house in Knoxville and moved there. In that first year, Tom Montelone, Stu's running friend from the Saratoga Stryders, invited us to have Christmas Dinner at his house and meet his family. He especially wanted us to meet Penny, Tom's wife's sister.

"Penny is a psychic," Tom said, when he introduced her to us. I'd never met a psychic before and had *never* believed in psychic powers. But I found myself telling Penny about Stu's stolen drawing, and his call to the psychic from North Carolina telling him that he "saw the women who stole it and that their artist friend was going to use Stu's drawing as a model to paint from and then destroy it.

Without missing a beat, Penny said sadly, "He did destroy it."

To this day, I have no idea if the psychic in North Carolina or Penny in Saratoga Springs could actually "see" what had taken place in Nashville in March of 1975. For all I know Stu's drawing might currently be hanging in somebody's house. All I know for sure is that we will never again see "Frog Girl & Friends."

Stu Runs

Stu races, showing
his usual intensity and focus.

The ancestors of mankind developed the
ability to run about four-and-a-half million years ago,
probably in order to hunt animals.

Stu doesn't hunt. The last time he'd raced was more than twenty years before when he was in the army and had become a member of a championship track team. In 1978, nine years after we'd moved to Knoxville, our city was chosen as the site of the 1982 World's Fair; the first ever to be held in the southeastern United States. They were inaugurating Expo 10,000, a six-mile road race, to publicize the World's Fair, and it enticed Stu back into competitive road running.

Although he had never run more than two miles before, Stu decided to compete in Expo. He was forty-six years old. With less than three weeks of training, he didn't really know if he could actually *run* for six miles. More than a thousand people participated in the race. By the time Stu crossed the finish line his tongue was hanging out. He didn't even check his finish time.

The following year Stu ran in Expo again. He wasn't yet a member of the Knoxville Track Club and only knew a few of the runners, but one of them suggested he check his finish time at the Athletic Center. When Stu gave the man his name, the guy congratulated him and handed Stu a trophy. He had come in fourth in his age group. From that moment on, Stu was hooked. For the next twelve years he usually came in first in his age category. Ten years after his first race, in 1988, the Knoxville Track Club chose Stu as their "Athlete of the Year"—and that included *all* age groups.

ATHLETE OF THE YEAR

The plaque was presented at their Annual Awards Banquet at the University of Tennessee Center. That plaque was the only one Stu wanted to keep when we moved to New York. He removed about a hundred-and-fifty others from the wall in our laundry room and took them to the Knox County dump.

Six years after receiving the Knoxville Track Club's "Athlete of the Year "award, Stu won first place in his age category in the "Run Fer the Hills 10K" finishing in Gatlinburg, Tennessee. The race took place on June 4, 1994, four days before Stu's 62nd birthday.

Athlete of the year plaque and another First Place win in Gatlinburg.

RUNNING TO WORK

Once a week for several months, Stu set the alarm for five in the morning and ran the eleven miles from our house to work. The day before he'd stash a change of clothes in the trunk, and leave his car in the parking lot overnight. One of the photographers who worked at the agency, lived about a mile past us. He'd drop Stu off at home on the evenings before he ran to work. (He also occasionally picked Stu up on his way *to* work when Stu's car ran out of gas on the Alcoa Highway.)

Lavidge & Associates had installed showers and dressing rooms that were often used by the models who did the TV and print commercials and, fortunately, by their creative director who ran to work once a week. After taking a shower on one of those "run to work" mornings, Stu called me at my office: "I have a group of high school students coming for a tour of the agency in forty-five minutes. After I got here I realized I didn't leave my suit pants with the rest of my clothes."

"Well, why don't you run home and get them," I said caustically. "Surely you don't think I'm going to leave work and bring them to you."

As it turned out, one of the agency's accounts was for boy's corduroy jeans. Stu found the largest size, with a 30" waist and squeezed into them. He has always been slender, but he later told me that for the entire time he wore those jeans he could hardly breathe.

That morning the group of high school students got an abbreviated tour of Lavidge & Associates.

STU DRIVES & RUNS IN SNOW

One day in early April as I left work for lunch, it had just begun to snow. I said to my lunch companion, "I'm going home." Knoxville, is in the foothills of the Great Smoky Mountains, and the roads are treacherous whenever it snows. I called Stu as soon as I got home and advised, "The smart money is home right now." He told me he'd leave when it started to get bad. I ate my lunch and decided to take a nap. When I woke up at almost four that afternoon, the sun was shining. I thought, *Uh oh, maybe it didn't snow much after all and I should have stayed at work.* However, looking out the window, I saw about a foot of snow covering the ground.

Stu arrived home at about 6:30. He'd left work at 2:30 and since it was almost impossible to drive, he decided to *run* home. He always carries his running clothes in the trunk of his car, so he parked near my office and changed into his running gear in the men's room. It had taken him more than two hours to get to my office from his—usually a twenty-minute drive. When he finally got home he told me that he was the only thing moving on the Alcoa Highway. Thinking he was out for a run, a few people trapped in stuck traffic, rolled down their windows and shouted things like "You asshole."

STU THE LEGEND

In May of 1994, sixteen years after competing in the first Expo 10,000, practically crawling across the finish line, Stu was trying for his 300th age-group title. A week before the race took place, the *Knoxville News-Sentinel* published the above story. Unfortunately, the day of the race the #2 Master runner in America had come from North Carolina to run in Knoxville's big race. Stu came in second; he said it wasn't even close. "That legend stuff must have angered the gods," I said.

TROPHIES

Stu had played tennis for years and was known as a player with a bad temper. After he started road racing, his temper improved radically—it's hard to throw a tantrum when you win. Soon he was winning a first place trophy practically every week—sometimes two a week if there were races on both Saturday and Sunday. Like a cat proudly showing off a dead mouse to its mate, my husband always left his trophy on the kitchen table for me to admire.

He then displayed all of them in floor-to ceiling bookcases in *my* studio. Individually, those little gold running figures are ugly, but in large groups they are dazzling. They sparkled in those bookcases until we moved to New York. The plaques, which Stu took to the dump, covered an entire wall—floor to ceiling—in the laundry-room.

Before we'd moved to Saratoga Springs in 2000, we knew there wouldn't be room in our new house for all those trophies.. An installation artist friend took the hundreds of trophies away in her van. Installation art is a three-dimensional work designed to transform the perception of a space; I could picture all those little gold figures running up a hill or disappearing down a sewer.

GOOD NEWS BAD NEWS

When Stu was in his mid-sixties, for the first time in his running career he started coming in second in his age group. Jack Ballard, a fat alcoholic who had lost more than a hundred pounds after he quit drinking and started running, was now coming in first. Ballard ran more than one-hundred-miles a week—a total fanatic, according to Stu: I thought: *you're the pot calling the kettle black.* I told Stu that we might have to hire a hit man to get rid of Ballard.

The week after I'd suggested that, Stu came home with another 2nd Place trophy. "Do you want the good news or the bad news?" he asked.

"The good news," I said.

"I had a pain in my chest during the race, but when I crossed the finish line right behind Ballard the pain went away." "I wouldn't call that *good* news," I said. "So what's the bad news?" "Ballard dropped dead on the way to his car with the 1st place trophy." I didn't say *anything.* Stu paused for a moment and said: "I'm not kidding. He really died. But, it could have been worse."

"How?" I asked. "He could have come in second."

STU SNOWSHOES

On February 12, 2011, Stu informed me that he was running in a snowshoe race. Rather than remind him that he'd never set foot in a snowshoe, I simply asked him if he was crazy. "I'll see how I like it," he blithely said as he left, blowing me a kiss while I gave him the finger. When he returned I asked how he did.

"I don't want to talk about it," he answered.

"You'll tell me eventually," I replied.

On Valentine's Day, before Stu handed me the box of Whitman's Chocolates that he usually eats himself, I asked when he was going to tell me about the snowshoe race. "I'll draw you a picture," he said. "The 'X' is where I went air-born. I crashed headfirst into a snow-bank. I was lucky it wasn't all ice or a tree," he said sheepishly.

I asked what he did after he landed. He told me he finished the race after he spit the snow out of his mouth and blew some more snow out of his nose. The entire incident made me furious. I had to stop myself from saying: "You should have blown it out your ass."

Stu finished his first and last snowshoe race in one hour, 27 minutes, and 19 seconds. He came in 160th out of 162 snowshoe racers. At seventy-eight, he was the oldest person and surely the only first-time snowshoe racer participating. Two middle-aged women finished last. I almost told Stu they'd probably stopped for coffee.

"You're actually lucky to be alive," I said wearily.

"I know. If I was a cat I'd have eight lives left."

"If you were a cat you'd already be dead," I replied.

Stu's hastily drawn card, was Scotch-taped to the box of candy. I wondered if he thought a red-snot heart coming out if his nose was a true expression of his love. Later that day I scanned his drawing, showing the "X" spot where he went airborne, and made my Valentine's Day card for hm.

110

Stu Runs Marathons

On October 18, 1987 Stu finished the
Detroit International Marathon in
3 hours, 8 minutes and 28 seconds.

Pheidippides, after running from
Marathon to Athens so he could announce the
Greek victory over Persia, dropped dead
on the spot from exhaustion.

Author Unknown

I have negative feelings toward running marathons, especially since I had known about Pheidippides' early death. I also believe that running twenty-six miles is a sign of insanity. When he was close to the age of fifty, Stu decided to train and try to qualify for the Boston Marathon. Four years after his first race in Expo, a six-mile race now seemed too easy.

STU QUALIFIES FOR BOSTON

To qualify for the Boston Marathon in his age group Stu needed to finish another marathon in less than three hours and thirty minutes. In October 1981, he ran in the Huntsville "Rocket City" Marathon in Alabama and crossed the finish line in three hours, two minutes, and 46 seconds. It was the best time he'd ever have. Stu has now run in nineteen marathons—including three times in Boston.

If Stu and I actually wanted to take part in the pre-marathon-carbohydrate-loading dinner, we needed to arrive at the high school gym in Huntsville by 6:00 P.M. the evening before the race. All those carbohydrates are supposed to help a person run a long distance race and dinner was also included in the race fee. They served as much spaghetti as one could possibly eat, lots of white rolls, and unlimited chocolate cake for the dessert. No salad. I went to all of these races with Stu. I told him that if he dropped dead like Pheidippides, I could strap him to the fender of the car, the way hunters do with a deer, and drive him home.

In the photo (below) of Stu crossing the finish line at the "Rocket City" marathon, I was the only person who was looking at him. Everyone near me was scanning the horizon, waiting for "their runner" to come in. When the clock over the finish line hit three-hours, even though I knew he'd qualified for Boston by almost half-an-hour, he wouldn't realize his dream of completing a marathon in less than three-hours, then or later, as it turned out.

Stu was disappointed with his time in Huntsville, even though he was way under the limit to qualify for Boston. I asked him if he thought he was from Krypton. As it turned out, after running in the Boston Marathon, he sadly admitted that he wasn't Superman after all.

HEAT WAS THE ENEMY

It was so hot in Boston the day of the marathon that a number of the almost 7,000 runners in the race didn't get to the finish line. Many of the top runners had skipped Boston in 1982 because they were in that year's Olympics. I planned to skip it also, because I wasn't feeling well, so Stu flew in the day before the race without me. He stayed with our friends Pat and Jerry Golden who had moved from Knoxville to Boston. I felt much better the following day, so I decided to fly to Boston. Stu, Pat, and Jerry were waiting at the airport to pick me up.

"Stu passed out after the race," Pat whispered to me.

"I'm glad I missed it then," I replied, shooting Stu a shocked look. The only other time he had passed out was before I knew him, when a podiatrist was cutting his ingrown toenail. The Boston Marathon doesn't start until noon, and Stu never eats anything before he runs. His blood sugar must have gone down to zero during the race. And by noon it was already over 80 degrees.

Also, Stu had never run in a race where he had to wait at least five minutes before even crossing the *starting* line. So to make up for the lost time he dashed in and out of the other runners, something he learned the hard way you don't do in a long race. He "hit the wall" after only eight miles, which usually happens to marathon runners only after 20 miles. He walked as much as he ran, and crossed the finish line in three hours and 47 minutes—a disgrace for Superman,

REDEEMING SUPERMAN

Stu ran Boston the second time on April 16th 1984 and redeemed Superman. I went along with him this time. It was cold, windy and raining. He finished in three hours-nineteen minutes, and fifty-eight seconds. After dinner we took the elevator to the sixth floor of our hotel and fell fast asleep. At two in the morning the fire alarm went off and we had to go down the stairs to the lobby in our nightclothes. It is extremely painful to go *down* steps after running a marathon. It was a false alarm. Don't ask why, but we stayed at the very same hotel four years later.

On April 18, 1988 Stu ran his third and last Boston Marathon in three hours, nineteen minutes, and 10 seconds. Not a bad time. At 1:30 that morning, the hotel fire alarm went off again. Even though it was another false alarm, we considered just ignoring the awful sound and covering our ears with pillows, but Stu said that maybe this time it really *was* a fire. So we once again descended the stairs in our nightclothes. However, twice in a row, that alarm felt like an omen. Although Stu ran in quite a few marathons after that, he never ran Boston again.

STU RUNS IN DETROIT'S INTERNATIONAL MARATHON

October 18, 1987 Stu ran in the *Detroit Free Press* International Marathon. What made it "International" was that the race started in Windsor, Canada, with the runners going through the Detroit-Windsor tunnel and ending up at Belle Isle Park, an island in the Detroit River.

Stu and I stayed at the Renaissance Center, a group of glass buildings on Detroit's riverfront. The Center's hotel looked beautiful on the outside, but had a dark depressing lobby. The Renaissance Center was meant to symbolize the hope that Detroit would soon experience its own rebirth. In 1956, the year we were married, Detroit was thriving. Now, much of the city is in ruins. On July 18, 2013, Detroit declared bankruptcy.

We'd spent our wedding night in Windsor, Canada. On December 28, 1956, the day after our wedding, Stu's mother's car, which she had lent us, broke down in the tunnel and we had to be towed out. Stu experienced that same sense of claustrophobia almost thirty years later, while running through the dimly lit and narrow tunnel during the *Detroit Free Press* International Marathon.

Stu's mother picked me up the morning of the race in front of the Renaissance Center. I couldn't believe that I would once again be a passenger in her car when, years before, I'd sworn I never would be. She drove to

Detroit's Belle Isle Park and we walked quickly to the finish line, where we waited for Stu to arrive.

He finished the race in three hours, eight minutes, and twenty-eight seconds. As soon as he could get out of the way, he lay down on the grass in pure exhaustion. It was his second best time in a marathon. And after the race, unlike Pheidippides, Stu lived to run another day.

Stu's Mother snapped the photo of me, the supportive wife, about two minutes after her son crossed the finish line.

Stu & Greta
Go to the Dogs

Six-foot-six-inch Stanley stands with
me and some of his dogs.

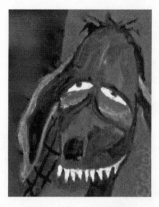

Irish Wolfhounds are the tallest dogs in the world.
An old Irish proverb describes the breed perfectly:
"Gentle when stroked, fierce when provoked."

We hadn't seen Stu's cousin, Stanley, since he was the lead story in the long-extinct "Divorce Column" of the *Detroit News*. The heading read: "Man Leaves Wife For Dogs." He'd divorced his wife of seven years, left his two children, moved to California, and married another dog-lover. Stanley was a year older than Stu—they had grown up together in Detroit, only one street apart—their mothers were sisters.

In the early sixties divorce was still considered a disgrace. After he shamed the entire family with his actions—not to mention the nasty story in the *Detroit News*—both sides of his family ostracized Stanley for many years; some never spoke to him again. But now, thirty years later, when Stu and I were in California for the first time, we stopped to see him.

In April of 1986, we flew to Los Angeles, CA from Nashville, TN, rented a car and drove along the Pacific Coast Highway to visit Stu's brother Marvin and his wife Marilyn in Danville—a bit east of San Francisco. From there, we planned to drive about 200 miles east to Yosemite National Park.

After a huge breakfast, as we were getting ready to leave, Marvin told us it wouldn't be that far out of our way to drive to where their cousin Stanley now lived. Stu called his cousin, and asked if we could stop by on our way to Yosemite. Stanley sounded really happy to hear from him.

GOING TO THE DOGS

When we got to Stanley's, he told us to hold tight to the railings of the porch. He was going to let the dogs out. Then ten enormous dogs came barreling out of his home like stampeding cattle.

Stanley and his second wife bred and raised Irish Wolfhounds. They made and sold their own "gourmet dog food," which they carefully prepared in their kitchen. On weekends they traveled in their large van to dog shows, where their gourmet dog food sold like hotcakes.

Cousin Stanley, who had grown up in a very nice house in Detroit, invited us in. We were stunned. The first thing that hit us was the smell of dog food cooking on the kitchen stove. Plastic sheets, covered with dog hair, protected the few pieces of furniture. There was not a single piece of art in the house, *nothing* on the dirty walls. Stanley asked us if we would like something to eat or drink. I truthfully told him that Marilyn had just served us an enormous breakfast. I didn't tell him that I, who had never been exceptionally fussy, wouldn't drink a glass of water in that house.

Stanley took us to see the kennel, which, compared to the house he now lived in, was spotless. As our mothers used to say: "You could eat off the floor." Ten Irish Wolfhounds accompanied us. I stroked them, as the old Irish proverb had advised, and saw only their gentle side. They totally ignored Stu, but seemed to like me and took turns licking my arms, my neck, and my face, which all became sticky with their affection.

THE WAITRESS

As soon as we'd said our goodbyes to Stanley and were back on the road, I told Stu that we'd have to stop at the first gas station or restaurant we came to so I could wash up. We soon found a small diner, where I went into the tiny bathroom, took off my T-shirt, and, using most of their soap and every one of their paper towels, removed all signs of the Wolfhounds' gentle fondness.

When I finally came out, Stu said that I had spent so much time in the diner's bathroom that we should probably eat something there. Although I wasn't at all hungry, knowing that Stu can never accept anything for free, I asked the waitress if we could split a grilled cheese sandwich and a small chocolate milkshake.

The waitress patted my recently scrubbed arm and said, "Honey, that will be just fine." A few minutes later she brought us two separate platters, each one holding a grilled cheese sandwich, French Fries, a bowl of Cole Slaw and a pickle. She put two chocolate shakes on the side.

"We were just going to split a regular grilled cheese sandwich and a small chocolate shake," I stammered.

"I always make too much," she replied, giving my arm another pat before walking away. Then I realized that she thought we were homeless since I had spent such a long time washing up in the bathroom.

I can never eat when I'm not hungry and all that food in front of me made me feel nauseated. Stu, who was really moved, after I told him the waitress thought we were homeless, ate everything in front of him and then some of mine. He drank both chocolate shakes.

When we paid the $4.20 charge with a $5 bill, Stu told the waitress to please keep the change. She asked us to wait just a minute and came back with a doggie bag packed with all our leftovers, plus some rolls, pats of butter, two paper plates, and plastic knives and forks. When I thanked her she simply patted my arm, surely thinking she was helping to feed the homeless. I didn't have the heart to tell her we were on vacation.

The doggie bag found a home in the first trashcan we came to. I'd had more than enough doggies for one day.

Stu & Greta's Worst Flight

Stu thought it was funny pretending
to be trapped in a bad motel. However,
there was nothing funny about being
trapped in an airplane.

In April 2010, the DOT issued a new rule
allowing passengers to deplane and
return to the gate in the event of a three-hour
or more delay on the tarmac.

The ruling by the Department of Transportation had come twenty-four years too late for us. In April 1986, Stu and I were flying from San Francisco, California to Nashville, Tennessee and then driving back home to Knoxville. The flights had cost us nothing, since Stu's brother Stanley had given us his frequent flyer miles on American Airlines, which unfortunately didn't fly out of the Knoxville airport. The day we left San Francisco I was wearing a short-sleeved T-shirt and light summer slacks. Stu wore shorts, because we knew it would be a lot warmer when we arrived back in Nashville.

Our wake-up call was at 6:00 A.M. We were in such a rush to return the rental car and get to the terminal on time that we didn't eat breakfast before we left. We expected to be served something resembling breakfast on the plane.

When we checked in for our 8:30 flight, the woman at the service desk told us our flight to Nashville had been cancelled. She apologized and then told us we had been rerouted through Chicago on a slightly later flight that would arrive in Nashville *earlier* than the cancelled flight. We walked quickly to the new gate, boarded at 8:55 and found our seats. We were due to arrive in Chicago at 1:10 that afternoon. Fifteen minutes after we were airborne the stewardesses served coffee, tea, and donuts.

THE FLIGHT FROM HELL

At about 1:30 the American Airlines pilot addressed the passengers on the intercom. He sounded annoyed. "Perhaps some of you have noticed that we've been circling Chicago for about an hour. I have some good news and some bad news. Actually, there is no good news. This plane is overloaded and we're running out of fuel. I knew we shouldn't have let you all on in San Francisco," he said sarcastically. "We will be making an emergency landing at Indianapolis Airport in exactly ten minutes." His intercom clicked off. The stewardess then said calmly, "Please fasten your seatbelts."

None of the 250 passengers seemed to panic. The plane landed at the very edge of the runway. A truck arrived and pumped in just enough jet fuel to circulate the air inside the plane; apparently we *had* run out of fuel. There was no food and soon enough nothing to drink—not even water. After the first couple of hours the toilets would not flush. Nobody was allowed to get off the plane. A few passengers, whose final *destination* was Indianapolis, were allowed off eight hours later. A small bus arrived along with aircraft steps, letting them climb down to the tarmac and be driven to the gate; however their luggage was going back to Chicago.

Stu and I both had books to read. Stu sat on the aisle and read until he finished his book. I was sitting in the center and had a harder time reading *my* book. Sitting at the window seat next to me was a young man from Taiwan who spoke broken English to me—non-stop—for hours. He had a pleasant, round face and a shy smile, which I would eventually grow to hate. It was his first trip to America and he was very excited to be on his way to Dayton, Ohio.

We had visited Stu's brother Stanley twice when his business relocated to Dayton for a few years, but I didn't tell the man from Taiwan that nobody in his right mind would want to go to what was possibly the dullest city in America. A classic headline from the *Dayton Daily News*: "OFF-DUTY DEPUTY HELPS NAB DAIRY QUEEN ROBBERY SUSPECT."

After several hours on the ground, the stewardesses were snapping at each other—something I'd never seen before. One of the pilots came out of the cockpit and was rude to a stewardess in front of the passengers. We learned why they were so upset when we finally arrived in Chicago.

Shortly after midnight, a stewardess addressed the passengers on the intercom. "We are now going to taxi to the terminal" she said, and everyone will be allowed to deplane." However, the stewardess warned, nobody should leave the gate area as our flight could be called to take off for Chicago at any time. At that point we had been sitting on the tarmac for almost eleven hours. Everyone got off except a very old man sleeping in first class and me, wanting nothing more than total silence. But eventually, I had to pee. I "deplaned" and dashed to the bathroom closest to the gate area. I waited in line for at least fifteen minutes.

However, as soon as I joined the crowd of unhappy passengers milling around the gate area, I couldn't find Stu. I did see the man from Taiwan standing alone; he actually looked happy to see the only person he knew. I asked him if he'd seen Stu. He pointed down the long passageway and said, "That way."

Right after he'd pointed to where Stu had gone, the announcement came over the loud speaker that we would be boarding immediately. I realized, of course, that I had no choice but to wait for Stu, and that we'd miss the flight. Suddenly I spotted him—a small figure running down the passageway carrying a very large bag. We got on the plane just in time for takeoff, and I waited to speak until we were sitting in our all-too-familiar seats. Thankfully, the man from Taiwan had fallen fast asleep, perhaps dreaming of Dayton. I was angry with Stu for leaving the gate and risking missing the flight to Chicago.

"What's that?" I asked, pointing to the enormous, greasy bag at his feet.

"It's popcorn," he said.

"I know it's popcorn, but what are you going to do with it?"

"Well, nobody has had anything to eat in hours and I thought I'd pass it around the plane."

"Popcorn makes a person really thirsty," I said snottily, "and there's nothing to drink on the plane." Stu reconsidered passing the popcorn around. He ate some and then asked me if he could put the bag next to me on the seat. I nodded and moved over as far as I could. The bag of buttered popcorn towered over me. Then Stu showed me his "Grand Prize." He had bought six candy bars and offered one to me. I declined.

There are times in a long-married couple's life when they just don't want anything to do with each other. This was absolutely one of those times. Stu ate a

Snickers bar while I closed my eyes. After that he ate a Mounds bar, and asked me what he should do with the wrappers. I told him to put them in the pocket in front of the seat with the vomit bag and all the magazines that he had already read twice. He informed me that the pocket was not a garbage bag and asked me to please put the candy wrappers in my purse. I was half-asleep. When I reached below my feet for my purse, the bag of popcorn flew into the air and rained popcorn on many of the passengers in front of us.

"Don't do that," Stu said very calmly and coldly to me.

"Let's start this conversation all over again," I said loudly. "You say, 'what should I do with these candy wrappers?' and I say, why don't you stick them up your ass."

Everyone within earshot heard me. Stu and I did not speak to each other all the way back to Chicago. When we finally deplaned, we learned there had been a severe thunderstorm that morning and a mid-sized passenger plane had crashed while trying to land at O'Hare; consequently all traffic at the busiest airport in America had to be diverted to other airports.

At O'Hare there were mobs of people sleeping on the floor. All the hotels were full and someone said it was *impossible* to get a cab to take us stranded passengers anywhere but downtown where all the hotel rooms were filled to capacity anyway. I got on an almost endless line to rebook our flight to Nashville. Stu had two cousins who lived in Chicago, so I told him to call Arnold who had stayed with us about a zillion times. But he wasn't home. So Stu called his cousin, Sonia. Her wonderful husband, Ray, answered the phone.

"Get a cab and come right over," he said and gave Stu their address. It was close to 1:30 A.M. I had booked our flight to Nashville for 12:30 P.M. the next day.

We left the airport without our luggage and tried to get a cab. Our bags, like us, were rerouted to Nashville. It was forty-five degrees outside and Stu and I were dressed in clothes appropriate for Nashville—not Chicago. We stood shivering as we tried to get a cab. None of the many cabs parked along the curb would take us to a residential neighborhood that late at night. Finally, one cabbie took pity on us. We arrived at Sonia and Ray's house at almost 2:30 in the morning and didn't even know if we were actually at the right place when I rang the doorbell. Fortunately, we were.

Sonia and Ray were both gourmet cooks. (Stanley, who cooked gourmet food for dogs, was Sonia's younger brother.) Sonia asked if she could fix us something to eat. Although I hadn't eaten anything but a donut in eighteen hours, I truly didn't feel hungry. Stu, who had recently eaten some greasy popcorn and two candy bars, declined. But then Ray said, "I just baked a big Marzipan Torte and made too much batter, so I made a little one. Would you like some?" *Maybe there* is *a God,* I thought and promptly ate the whole thing.

Every Thanksgiving, Ray brought his Marzipan Torte to the family reunion. It is the most delicious cake I have ever tasted. Once, on their way from Chicago to Florida, Sonia and Ray visited us in Knoxville. I had invited them to have dinner and sleep over. Ray carried what I thought was the most peculiar piece of luggage I had ever seen. It turned out to be a portable refrigerator holding a huge Marzipan Torte he'd baked just for me. Luckily, Stu hates Marzipan. I cut it into pieces and froze most of it, thinking I would invite friends over one day to taste it. However, I never did share it with anyone.

After surviving the flight from hell, we went to bed in Sonia and Ray's guest bedroom. Sonia lent me a nightgown and Stu slept in his underwear. We fell asleep the moment we hit the bed. The next day Sonia made us breakfast and Ray drove us to the airport. He and I were always simpatico. We had each married into the same crazy family.

Ray's Marzipan Torte.

Stu Goes
Back to College

Stu stands between two oil paintings
he completed when he was a student at
The University of Tennessee
College of Art.

In 1991 Stu was almost sixty.

At the time the United States was founded,
average life expectancy at birth was only 35 years.
It reached 47 years in 1900, jumped to 68 years in 1950
and steadily rose to 76 years in 1991.

Stu often changed jobs during his twenty-five year career in advertising. However, whether he was an Art Director on Madison Avenue, or the Creative Director at two different advertising agencies in Knoxville, did he ever work on *any* job for more than five years. Some jobs lasted just a couple of days—or hours. He either quit or was fired.

In 1991, Stu quit advertising for good and enrolled as a freshman at the University of Tennessee's College of Art. He had always wanted to be a painter when he grew up. Most of "the kids," his fellow students, were right out of high school. They naturally assumed that Stu was the teacher since he was almost sixty years old.

Now back in school, Stu remembered absolutely nothing from the single oil-painting class he had taken at Pratt more than thirty years before. He needed to relearn how to work with oils—even how to mix the paints. Not wanting to be embarrassed when he once again became an art student, he enrolled in a two-week summer workshop at the Arrowmont School of Arts and Crafts. Arrowmont, a national art education center nestled in the Smoky Mountains of Gatlinburg, TN, was an hour-and-a-half's drive from our house in Knoxville.

STU LEARNS TO MIX PAINT

The two-week workshop fee included three meals a day and sleeping quarters in the dorm. It was, however, too hot and very noisy in the dorm, so Stu drove home late every night to our air-conditioned and peaceful house and left early each morning. When the workshop ended, he brought home the five oil paintings he had finished and lined them up on the front porch for me to see. "Put them all directly in the garbage," I said. "Don't even think about bringing them into the house."

"You don't like them?" he said, sounding completely astonished. Stu and I had both graduated from Pratt Institute. We both had good careers as artists and were always honest, sometimes brutally honest, about each other's work. "I think they're truly awful," I said.

Four immediately went into the trash. For some crazy reason Stu kept one—a ghastly painting of a cow's skull, in the garage. The cow's skull eventually joined the other four paintings to decompose in some landfill.

STU PAINTS

After his first week as a student at the University of Tennessee, Stu brought me to the university studio late one evening to look at his first painting. He didn't want any of the other students to overhear my comments.

"Holy shit!" I said. "That is gorgeous. You're going to be a painter."

Stu's first of many oil paintings.

129

Stu had always worked on small pieces in a "tight" style. His layouts for advertising were never larger than a full-page newspaper ad. He rarely used color. His black and white pencil drawings were on 18 x 24 inch pieces of paper. And now, to my amazement, he was working with brilliant colors on a five by four-foot canvas that he had stretched himself.

Stu's first painting was abstract, probably because he started where he had left off in the fifties—when abstract expressionism was what most artists were creating. But when he went back to college more than thirty years later, even though he continued painting some large abstracts, he started working in different styles, sizes, and materials. After all, school is a time to experiment.

GRANDFATHERING MATH

All the students in the Bachelor of Fine Arts program at the University of Tennessee were required to take specific academic subjects such as art history, a foreign language, and math as well as their art courses. The university accepted the credits Stu had earned at Pratt, in courses including English, Psychology, Great Books, and History of Art. However Pratt did not oblige the art students to take math, or Stu would never have graduated. Pratt understood that art students usually do poorly in math. The lone foreign language he'd ever studied was Hebrew for his Bar Mitzvah. The only words the Hebrew teacher said directly to him were in English: "Shut your mouth Mr. Eichelbaum or leave the room."

After Stu enrolled at UT, an official summoned him to his office to schedule the academic classes that he would need to pass in order to graduate. But Stu told him that he absolutely would *not* take math, explaining that he was almost sixty years old and if he had lived that long and didn't need math he doubted he would ever use it in the future. He would be willing to study Spanish if he had to take a foreign language, because he might possibly use it someday.

After consulting with the Dean of the College of Art, the official told Stu that he would be "Grandfathered" in both math and learning a foreign language. He explained that "Grandfathering" basically means that someone is exempt from any new requirements based on "certain" criteria. Stu said it was certain that he would fail math. I agree. It is also certain that Stu, who does not think sequentially, could ever have learned a foreign language. He can, however, do a perfect imitation of any accent on the planet.

STU SCULPTS

At Pratt, Stu had never become proficient in three-dimensional design. Now, back in college, he studied both sculpture and ceramics. Stu found he could not operate a potter's wheel and almost everything he fired in the kiln either cracked or exploded. But he doesn't give up easily.

One evening he arrived home from his sculpture class looking despondent—almost ill.

"What's the matter?" I asked. "Are you alright?"

"Dracula wouldn't fit in the coffin," he said sadly, not realizing I had no earthly (or unearthly) idea of what he was talking about. It seemed Stu had done a sculpture of Dracula in his coffin, the lid warning: DON'T OPEN IN DAYLIGHT. After removing all three pieces from the kiln, the lid fit perfectly, but Dracula, exhibiting yet another annoying characteristic, refused to go down quietly. Eventually Stu prevailed by filing down his legs.

Dracula rests uneasily in his coffin.

The first assignment in ceramics was to craft a vase. Since the potter's wheel was out of the question, Stu prepared his vase by stacking coils of clay of various lengths on top of each other. Then he cut out a window so that an apparently bored clay woman could look outside. The first assignment for sculpture was to create a lamp. Stu molded a figure with his hands and inserted the metal tube provided by the teacher into the soft clay before firing it.

Both the vase and the lamp cracked in the kiln, but Stu glued each of them back together. He then threaded an electric cord through the tube in the body of his clay-man lamp and used a light bulb for its head. We bought red tulips for the vase and a green shade for the lamp. I worried about plugging it into an electrical outlet, afraid that any lamp made by Stu could burn down the house.

STU SCULPTS SHIT

The assignment for the senior sculpture students was to create something that would almost force a person, if only out of sheer curiosity, to pick it up. Stu coiled strips of clay to resemble a pile of dog-shit, painted it dark brown and stuck a shiny piece of fake gold in it, before putting his creation into the kiln. The pile of shit was the only one of his sculptures that didn't blow up or crack.

An assistant professor in the art department always brought her small dog to class. Sometimes her pet would be the model for her students to draw. One morning when she entered the Art and Architecture building with her dog on its leash, Stu said, "Look what your dog just did!" Not noticing the shiny piece of gold in it, she said coldly to Stu, "He never does that." Stu picked up the pile and showed her that it was really a sculpture. After shooting him an I'd-really-like-to-kill-you look, she gave her dog's leash a little tug and quickly walked away. After that day she never spoke to Stu again.

When I opened the refrigerator door that evening the shit-sculpture was on the top shelf. I didn't mention it to Stu, but left it in his underwear drawer. He put it in the toaster oven. I left it on the front seat of his car.

We soon grew tired of this game, so we wrapped the shit-sculpture in toilet tissue, stuck it in a box, put it on a closet shelf and quickly forgot all about it—until our son Steven came to visit for the weekend. He mentioned that he'd recently swallowed the gold crown for his back molar and the dentist told him that he needed to "pass it." He told our son that as soon as he "passed" the crown to come to his office and he would then sterilize it and glue it back in his mouth.

Naturally, Stu immediately retrieved his pile-of-shit-with-the-gold-piece sculpture from the closet. Steven, whose sense of humor is the same as his father's, brought it to his dentist the following Monday. The dental group was having their Monday morning meeting when Steven knocked on the door before walking right in and pulling his daddy's sculpture out of his pocket.

"I passed the gold tooth," he said happily, before handing it to Dr. Phillips.

After a brief pause, every dentist in the room almost fell on the floor laughing. Dr. Phillips asked Steven if he could keep the sculpture, because he wanted to tell the story at dental conventions.

STU IN A SHOE

Combining what he'd learned in sculpture, ceramics and photography, Stu fashioned a figure of himself driving a running shoe. After gluing the figure back together after it cracked in the kiln, placing it in an old running shoe, and wrapping the laces around wires to make them appear to be flying, he then took photos of his creation in various death-defying situations.

Top left: The Grim Reaper closes in. Top right: Over the cliff.
Bottom left: Emerging from a dark place. Bottom right: Parking in a tight spot.

STU & . . .

When Stu handed in the first assignment for his senior watercolor class, the teacher burst out laughing. "I can't wait to see what you do next," he said. Stu had no thought at the time of creating a series that would turn into twenty paintings, three solo shows, and become known as "Stu & . . ."

Stu meets with Stalin, Roosevelt & Churchill in 1943.

Stu spent hours in the library. It took a lot of research for him to find just the right photo of every person he wanted to paint. Before starting the painting of him performing with Elvis Presley, we had to borrow a guitar from a friend. I took a photo of Stu with an intense expression on his face performing Elvis' hip-thrusting movement. I woke him up at four in the morning to tell him he needed to paint "Stu & Elvis" on black velvet.

"That's a disgusting idea," he said, only half awake. "Go back to sleep."

But when he asked the other students what they thought about painting him and Elvis on black velvet, they agreed with me. Stu then bought a large piece of velvet and stretched it onto a six-foot-wide frame. The velvet "ate the paint," so Stu needed to paint over the same areas many times. It was worth it. "Stu & Elvis" on black velvet appeared to glow from within.

Top: Elvis, in his "getting fat phase" doesn't seem to like Stu's performance.
Above left: Stu walks with Albert Einstein as the Atomic Bomb explodes.
Right: A photo of Stu standing in front of Stu & Albert."

For each of his "Stu &" paintings, I photographed him wearing the "Stubbed Toes" tee shirt that he'd designed as a joke for him and some of his running friends. He always wore light brown corduroy slacks and his Nike running shoes.

Stu also painted himself being interviewed by Larry King with his feet up on Larry's desk; walking down a cobblestone street holding Frankenstein's hand; cutting in on Rhett Butler waltzing with the recently widowed Scarlet O'Hara; cavorting with Snow White and the

Seven Dwarfs; having Jackson Pollack fling paint all over his "Stubbed Toes" tee-shirt; holding a gold bible while saving both Jim and Tammy Baker; standing at attention, with his hand over his heart, next to the crisply saluting General George Patton, both standing in front of an enormous American flag. And there's more . . .

STU & JEFFREY

Stu would never tell me, unless he absolutely had to—such as when he needed to borrow a guitar from a friend of mine for his Elvis painting—what he was going to paint next. He wouldn't even tell me after I'd helped him get the props and taken his photo. He liked to surprise me.

One evening he said we had to buy a Honeydew melon and a head of lettuce. When we brought them home from the supermarket, Stu asked me to show him how to put lettuce leaves on a plate. After putting the Honeydew melon on the lettuce, clutching a knife and fork, with a demonic look on his face he pretended to be devouring the melon.

"Are you eating Jeffrey Dahmer's head?" I asked, incredulous that he would even think of painting, no less eating, the head of the infamous serial killer and cannibal.

"How did you guess?" he asked, sounding amazed.

"I've been married to you for almost forty years," I said. Then he finished his painting of "Stu & Jeffrey," replacing the placeholder-melon with Jeffrey Dahmer's head.

"I really don't think you need to paint Jeffrey Dahmer or even show a painting like that to anyone. It's totally disgusting. It's not *anything* like your painting 'Stu & Frankenstein', I insisted. "Dahmer is a *real* monster."

Stu ignored my plea. He told me he was going to put all of the "Stu &" paintings in his upcoming show at Gallery 1010, the College of Art's student gallery. All seniors in the program were encouraged to exhibit their work at Gallery 1010 before graduation.

Stu brought photos of his "Stu &" paintings to *The Knoxville News-Sentinel*, showed them to a staff writer, and asked if he would be interested in writing a story about the show. The editorial staff loved the idea and published a full-page article the day before the opening.

"'Stu & Jeffrey' is my favorite painting," a man told Stu, at the opening reception. Stu then glanced at me smugly and said, "Thanks. My wife didn't want me to include it in the show."

"I think she was right," the man said.

Stu needed only three more credits to get a Bachelor of Fine Arts degree from the University of Tennessee. He never bothered. Although I knew he already had a BFA from Pratt, I asked, "Why don't you just take a three-credit class and get the degree?"

Stu replied, "Having two Bachelor degrees is about as useful as having two assholes."

Stu & Small Creatures

Stu had never shown positive feelings for ants, mice, sparrows, crickets, snakes, frogs, or the creature seemingly controlling his computer.

I'm truly sorry man's dominion
Has broken Nature's social union,
An' justifies that ill opinion . . .

Robert Burns

When Stu was a child, he was never big enough to be "King of the Hill," where winning could be achieved only by knocking the previous kid-king off the top. So he would find an anthill and pretend he was God—an unmerciful God, who could wipe out an entire city with his foot.

An ant colony is a subterranean dwelling where ants live, eat, and tend the eggs produced by their Queen. The worker and soldier ants are in charge of taking care of and defending the city of ants and bringing food to the queen in her elite Queen-of-the Anthill-quarters. There are rooms for nurseries and food storage, all built and maintained by the legions of worker ants. Sort of like our own world.

When Stu stomped on the city, he watched as thousands of worker ants scurried to escape his wrath— deserting their queen. If he was in a really bad mood, he became a cruel God who destroyed the fleeing ants before any refugee camps could be found.

STU, THE MOUSE, & ME

Stu hates mice. Like my Grandma, who flushed my pet mouse down the toilet saying it was a baby rat, Stu would have done the same. Grandma died when I was seventeen, the year before I met my future husband.

During the three years that Stu and I were living in my parents' basement, we went upstairs each weekday night to watch the Ben Hecht Show on television, which started at 11:15 P.M. Promptly, at 11:20 P.M. a little gray mouse came out of hiding and paraded across the living room while we watched TV. My mother had tried for months to catch it in a trap under the kitchen sink, but that mouse was too smart to touch the cheese.

One night I watched it go up the steps that led to the bedroom where my mother and father were by then sound asleep. The mouse had slipped between the tread and the riser of the carpet that ran up the steps, so I placed a foot on each side of the stair step—effectively trapping it. Thinking I was smarter than the mouse, I shouted triumphantly to Stu: "Quick! I've got it." Then, lowering my voice so as not to wake my parents: "Get a broom from the closet and a paper bag." Stu, mystified, did as I asked.

"Now watch," I said patiently, "I'm going to move the mouse to the left with my right foot. When I say 'Now!' you hit it with the broom and then sweep it into the paper bag. If it's still alive we'll let it out the front door. Ready?" Stu said he was ready, tentatively holding the broom and the paper bag.

I slowly moved the mouse under the carpet to the very edge of the stair. I whispered as quietly as I could, "Now!" When the little creature dashed out I watched the broom fly in one direction, the paper bag in an-other and Stu in still another. The mouse quickly vanished and was smart enough never again to join us for Ben Hecht's Show. I'm sure that mouse eventually died of old age.

STU AND THE SNAKE

Stu called me at work from home one day. He'd recently quit advertising to become a full-time painter. "There's a big black snake in our living room. I don't know what to do. Should I hit it with an axe?" he said, with a touch of panic in his voice. I had recently redone the living room using white carpeting.

"If you hit a snake with an axe on my new white carpeting I will come home and hit *you* with an axe," I said. "Let me ask Hugh Bailey what to do." Hugh, a fellow artist who worked in the office next door to mine, had grown up on a farm and knew all sorts of things about wildlife. "Ask Stu what it looks like," Hugh suggested. After Stu described it to me, Hugh said it was probably just a garter snake and isn't poisonous.

"Tell Stu to get a paper bag and a broom and to guide the snake into the bag. Then just take it outside, open the bag and let it out." Déjà vu. I had to repress a laugh remembering the appearance of the Ben-Hecht-viewing mouse in my parents' living room in Brooklyn. Somehow, although I told Stu what Hugh's instructions were, I couldn't believe he would actually follow them.

When I arrived home that evening, Stu proudly told me that he had done what Hugh said to get rid of the snake. He had guided it into a paper bag and let it out in the woods across the street. I congratulated him, but I knew he thought I didn't *really* believe him.

Actually, what I didn't believe was the snake was as long as he'd described, that it was probably just a cute little baby snake which I probably would have picked up with my hands and tossed outside. I was never afraid of snakes, mice or bugs.

When I got home the following night, Stu told me that the big black snake had returned. He was going into his painting studio, which was connected, to our garage, which was connected to our house, when he saw it in the garage. He didn't get a broom and a paper bag and catch the snake as he had told me successfully done the day before. Neither did he kill it with an axe on the carpet-less garage floor as he'd suggested he could do the day before. He took a photo of it instead.

I think Stu just wanted to *prove* to me how long the snake really was. The last time he saw it, the snake was slithering into a hole in the wall, never to appear again. Although we still have the photo, I can't find it. It is lost somewhere in my closet. Like the real snake we will probably never see it again.

The only creature that Stu dislikes even more than a snake or a mouse is the mouse that determines, as if on its own, what happens on his computer. It is an enemy often worthy of being hit with a broom, swept into a paper bag, and thrown out the front door.

STU, THE SPARROW & THE CRICKET

A cricket left our house unwillingly the other night. Stu had stomped on it three times, and when it didn't seem to be dead, he put it outside. He pretended to feel rotten, made a long face, and said he wished he had stepped on it only *once* before putting it outside when it might have had a better chance to survive. I asked him if he wanted to take it to the vet.

It reminded me that more than thirty years ago, on our way to dinner at a restaurant we saw a sparrow standing on our lawn next to the path. Although we walked right past it, it didn't fly away. By the time we arrived home it was lying on its back—still alive, but just barely. We put the sparrow in a shoebox and ten minutes later, we arrived at the Veterinary Hospital.

Before the vet's assistant would take responsibility for the bird's welfare, she asked for Stu's name, address and phone number. She also handed him a release to sign. When Stu realized she wasn't kidding, he said he wanted *them* to sign a paper promising not to perform any kind of cruel scientific experiment on the sparrow. They ignored him. Stu signed the release and gave them the bird. I didn't call the school later that evening to see how the sparrow was doing. The stupid bird was probably already dead.

I already had some prior experience with the College of Veterinary Medicine. As a publications artist for the University of Tennessee I had designed a lot of jobs for them. One year, I'd created a cover for their recruiting publication, which had something to do with growth and a nest. I arranged for a photograph to be taken of a bird's nest in which I placed four hard-boiled eggs that were dyed light blue.

The Media Relations people at the vet school said the cover was beautiful but they couldn't use it. They would have to prove that the eggs weren't *viable*; that the hatchling chicks inside could not have survived. I had to stop myself from asking whether they were part of some "Right Wing" organization.

Instead I said, "They're chicken eggs, you know—the kind you scramble. "

It made no difference to them. Rules are rules.

THE EYES HAVE IT

The mechanic who fixes our car also photographs small creatures. He offered to trade Stu one of his photos for one of Stu's paintings. Stu gave him a painting of an old car and brought home a photo of a tree frog, which we immediately hung in our kitchen.

Stu kept looking at that photo as if he had never seen a frog before. "God, it's so human," he said. "Its eyes seem to be looking right at me. It really looks like it's smiling." That frog has almost become a member of our family.

When Stu was in the army he said he could never kill someone who was looking at him. Maybe because the mouse and the sparrow could have been looking at him he was loath to be responsible for their deaths. His computer mouse will always be in danger. Snakes, crickets and ants don't count—you can't see their eyes. However, any frog on the planet will be safe around Stu.

Photo by Gary Childs.

Stu & Music

Singing as one of "The Three Tenors"
Stu donned a suit jacket over his tee shirt.
When I took his picture, he was
singing "Happy Birthday"—the only song
for which he knew all the words.

*"The only escapes from the miseries
of life are music and cats . . ."*
Albert Schweitzer

Unlike Albert Schweitzer, in order to escape *his* childhood miseries, Stu stepped on ants. And neither he nor his twin brother Edward had ever shown the *slightest* interest in music. (Stu also hated cats.) They were visual artists from the time they were old enough to hold pencils. Stu told me that his parents never listened to music in their house—they didn't even have a record player. My parents owned the entire set of 78 RPM classical records put out by *The Herald Tribune,* and they listened to music every night.

THE FAMILY VIOLIN

Stu's family was not musical, but somehow, one of his mother's relatives brought a "family violin" with them when they came to America from the Ukraine. It was passed around to all the children, but none of them took to playing it. When Stu was about nine-years old, it was his turn. His mother found a violin teacher to give her twin sons lessons. Edward refused to even *try.* After Stu's first lesson his teacher asked him to promise never to touch a violin again as long as he lived.

NOT SINGING IN THE CHORUS

When Stu was in the 8th grade, his friend, Hershel Plotnick, thought it would be fun if they joined the chorus. In the nearly six decades I've known him, the only song I ever heard Stu sing was "Happy Birthday," and not very well at that.

At James Madison High, where I sang in the Girl's Chorus, we were all petrified of Mrs. Stein, the choral director. I have heard, for some yet undisclosed reason, choral directors frighten their students.

Stu's choral teacher terrified him. One afternoon, adeptly mingling resignation with disgust, she tapped her baton on the music stand, and said,

"Only one student has not looked at me even *once* during this entire class: Stuart Eichelbaum."

"He wasn't singing either," his good friend Hershel Plotnick announced.

CONCERT VERSUS BOXING

When Stu and I first started dating, I suggested we go to a concert. I told him I used to play the piano. At the beginning of our relationship, I didn't yet know that on a scale of one to ten, his fondness for classical music was zero.

One day, he asked me to go to a boxing match with him, telling me he used to box. I said I despised boxing, and that I never even stayed in the same *room* when my father watched the "Friday Night Fights" on television. Stu insisted boxing was a science; I felt boxing was a holdover from the Roman Coliseum—only people had replaced the lions.

"Let's make a deal," Stu said. "You go to a boxing match with me and I promise to take you to whatever concert you'd like to go to."

"It's a deal," I replied cautiously. I'd never seen live boxing. Not that long after this, we went to a boxing match at Madison Square Garden and sat too close to the ring. I almost threw up when blood began to gush from one of the combatant's nose.

Forty years later, after moving to Saratoga Springs, we went to hear the Philadelphia Orchestra play at the Saratoga Performing Arts Center. We sat up close and Stu did quick sketches of members of the orchestra.

"Don't ever say I didn't keep my promise," he said.

Now, having been in Saratoga Springs for fifteen summers in a row, Stu *almost* likes going to see the Philadelphia Orchestra's performances, although he enjoys the New York City ballet a lot more. During the concerts he likes *watching* the musicians and the conductor, practically dancing on the podium.

THE SOUND OF PIANO MUSIC

Stu's favorite musical of all time is "The Sound of Music." The sound of a piano, however, was a different story. I played the piano from the age of five until I was fifteen. I practiced every day for an hour. In my second year of high school, I quit. There was just too much homework to do, plus I had started dating.

I married Stu when I was nineteen. As I've surely mentioned before, as students at Pratt we lived in my parents' basement. The piano, of course, was upstairs. Whenever Stu and I had a really *nasty* argument, we'd clam up and not speak to each other. I would usually go upstairs and take my fury out on the piano.

For years after moving out of my parents' basement, Stu refused to have a piano in the house. I couldn't blame him. He associated the sound of piano music with anger—a genuine Pavlovian response. The sound of a barking dog drives *me* crazy, but Stu doesn't even *hear* it.

By 1963 we'd been married for seven years, had two children, and lived on the sixth floor of an apartment house complex in Howard Beach, NY. I wanted to get a piano, but Stu wouldn't hear of it. Pavlov's dog was still alive and well in his head. So I went across the hall, where my new friend, Terry, let me play her piano any afternoon I felt like it. My children napped on her kids' beds. She listened to me for as long as I wanted to play, or until Steven or Ellen woke up.

Stu was embarrassed that Terry knew I'd played for so many years yet didn't have my own piano. On February 14,1964, two men delivered my Valentine's Day present—a beautiful Story & Clark upright piano. They turned it on its side in the small elevator, wheeled it to our apartment at the very end of the hall on the sixth floor and set it up in our living room. I had no idea that Stu had bought it for me. I wept. I played it every day before he came home from work.

PIANO LESSONS

Two years later, we moved into our first house in Huntington Station, New York. I wanted Steven, who was then six, to take lessons from our piano teacher friend across the street. Stu asked Steven if he would rather take piano lessons or tennis lessons. Sensing his father's preference, he chose tennis.

Steven is now married with two children of his own. Michaela, when she was eight-years-old, started taking piano lessons; now she is ten and has mercifully been allowed to quit. Jordana, who is now eight, will get the chance to take lessons if she really *wants* to.

Listening to Michaela struggling to play something for us while we were visiting, Steven asked me why we never gave *him* piano lessons.

"Why don't you ask your father?" I said.

Stu Paints In Open Air

The above photo of Stu painting
the Schaghticoke Fire Department's
1895 building appeared
in the *Troy Record*.

"Plein air painters are advised to scout out locations before they decide where to set up their easel. They are advised to look around 360 degrees so they don't miss the possibilities behind them."

Marion Boddy-Evans

ATTACKED BY A ROOSTER

Stu came home one evening after a day of painting on a farm with a large bloody gash on his leg. A rooster had attacked him with its spur. As part of a backyard flock, roosters can be dangerous because an aggressive one uses his spurs, a sharp, bony projection on his legs, as a weapon. During most of the day the rooster sits on a high perch, to serve as a lookout for his flock. He will sound his distinctive alarm call if predators are nearby and charge through the yard like a bull.

Stu didn't know any of this the day he was painting a barn and nearby a rooster started jumping up and down. He thought the rooster was just showing off like an annoying kid trying to get an adult's attention when they're busy. So Stu just ignored the angry rooster and wanted to say to it, "I don't have time for this shit. Go find your mother and jump around for her." Stu hesitantly told the farmer that his rooster had attacked him. Stu hates to complain to the farmers fearing they won't want him to return.

"You're lucky it wasn't the damn geese," the farmer warned. "They're meaner." The following day Stu told me he was going back to the same place to finish his painting. I objected. "What about that rooster?" I asked.

"Don't worry. I know how to deal with roosters now," he said. "Like how?" I wondered aloud.

"I'll jump up and down and make a noise just like he does," Stu explained patiently.

"Sounds like a cockfight to me," I said assuredly, as if I'd actually seen one.

TRIPPING ON A TILLER

Plein air painting does have its dangers. Painters in the open air have sometimes fallen off cliffs, been struck by lightning, attacked by bears, and occasionally hit by trucks, among other catastrophes. Stu's risks have not been quite that dramatic, (except for that angry rooster) but some of them could have been life threatening—like the time he tripped over a tiller.

When Stu is painting outside, he often doesn't notice what's behind him. While doing an oil painting of a red truck, he backed up to admire his work and tripped over a tiller—a long, sharp piece of farm equipment that turns the soil and mixes it with manure. That machine was right behind him, and he had previously left his can of Diet Coke on it, but then quickly forgot about the tiller being there.

I knew something was wrong when Stu didn't call me on his cell phone to let me know what time he'd be home. When he didn't show up for dinner, I went ahead and ate my own dinner, thinking if I needed to go to the hospital or to the morgue there was no point in being hungry.

STU CALLS FROM THE EMERGENCY ROOM

Just as I was finishing dessert, Stu called me from the ER and told me not to worry. He was all right, but the emergency room doctor needed to know if he'd had a tetanus shot last year when he was attacked by the rooster. He had.

Stu had a nasty gash on his forehead from falling on the tiller and needed nine stitches. His little finger was badly dislocated—it *looked* broken and had turned purple and blue, with a touch of green. He had bruises all over his body. He'd finished his painting with blood dripping onto his glasses. Then he took a photo of it on the easel with the real red truck in the background. He later told me that reason he felt he needed to finish the painting right away was because he thought; *Greta will never let me come back here (*as if I had a choice). Only then did he drive forty minutes to Saratoga Hospital.

PAINTING, AND ALMOST BUYING, THE FARM

Stu often paints on farms. When he sees something he likes, usually looking over his left shoulder while he's driving on some curvy road, he stops and honks his horn. If nobody comes out of the house, he sets up his easel and starts painting. He normally didn't knock on people's front doors because some old guy in a tank top and shorts showing up uninvited could frighten *anyone*, much less an elderly widow who might be inside the farmhouse. If someone eventually comes out to see what he's been doing, the painting usually delights them and later Stu sends them a print of it and writes a note of thanks. One day a kid sitting outside told Stu that they have all the paintings [prints] framed in their house and they've saved all his notes.

Most of the farmers like the idea of Stu painting on their land, but a few are not happy to have him on their property. One irate farmer asked Stu if he could *read*

while he was painting an old truck ten feet inside a fence with a six by eight foot NO TRESPASSING sign clearly displayed on it. The farmer refused to believe that Stu didn't see the sign, but I *know* he didn't. Stu focuses so intently on his subject that most of the time he doesn't notice anything else. The irate farmer let Stu finish his painting. Another farmer threatened to shoot him if he didn't get off his land. This seldom happens, but after being shooed off yet one more farm by a young man wearing camouflage attire and obviously suffering from Post Traumatic Stress Disorder, Stu realized he would, in the future, have to ask for permission before he started to paint.

Stu arrived home one evening and showed me his latest painting of a wonderful old red truck. The only problem was that farm was protected by an electric fence. The owners of the farm had to leave early, and the man told Stu he'd show him how to lock up and reactivate the fence. I couldn't stop laughing. I told Stu it was an absolute miracle he didn't electrocute himself. Obviously, the farmer had no idea with whom he was dealing.

For his next subject Stu chose a beautiful old yellow barn covered with vines. The farmer said he would be happy to have him paint it. When he arrived the next day, all those interesting vines, which attracted him to paint it in the first place, had been removed. Stu then painted what he told me was a "naked barn," so as not to hurt the farmer's feelings

Left: Naked Barn with permission. Right: Tractor without permission.

GOT MILK?

Every Sunday, when Stu still ran ten miles in the countryside, he passed a dairy farm and always said to the cows lined up in their stalls, "Got milk?" "They never answer, they only smile," Stu told me. Cows, as opposed to roosters, are not aggressive. They are friendly and curious. When they see Stu painting in a field they will sometimes stop eating the grass and watch him paint. The only thing he has to worry about is, if he lets them come too close, they'd put their noses in his paint pallet.

STU EICHEL DISCOVERS LAND

Stu usually included *some* kind of landscape in the background of his paintings, but always needed to have something man-made as the subject: a truck; an old car; a tractor; a barn; a fake cow. Recently he came home with a *landscape*. My first (and last) mate had spotted land. Landscapes ahoy!

Off Stafford Bridge Road in Saratoga County.

OF Wagaman Ridge Road in Washington County.

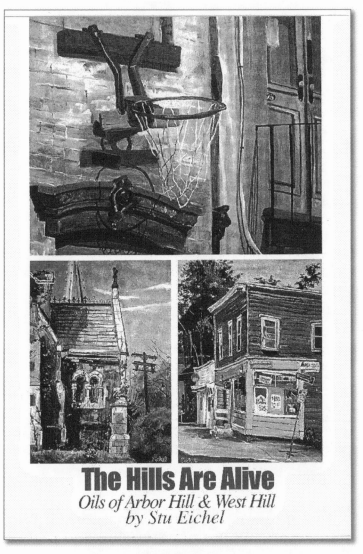

The Hills Are Alive
*Oils of Arbor Hill & West Hill
by Stu Eichel*

Stu Paints "The Hills"

*Arbor Hill is 88% Black, 6% Latino, 4% Multiracial,
1% White, and 1% Asian. 73% of students are
eligible for the free lunch program.*

N.Y. State Report Card

*"West Hill and Arbor Hill are the two worst neighborhoods in
Albany. But as long as you don't try and mess with
drug dealers, you should be okay."*

Posted online 2/23/09 by wendywanderer

*Hamilton Hill, Schenectady's grittiest neighborhood,
is just six-tenths of a square mile but it accounts
for half of the gunfire reported in the city.*

Lydia Polgreen / The New York Times

Stu fell in love with "The Hills" when some selected artists in the Capital Region were invited by the Albany County Historical Association to create paintings of buildings that had been abandoned and boarded up. The Historical Association was planning a fundraising exhibit they'd titled, "Vacancy." The paintings would be auctioned off and the money would be used to restore some of the beautiful old buildings.

"You ain't afraid to be in the 'Hood', are you?" a large black man said one day, standing over Stu while he painted. "Not at all," Stu replied. "I've been treated very well by everyone here." That was true. The people in the "Hood" were more interested in his work than people had been in places where he had painted before.

Neighborhood residents offered him bottled water to drink. They brought their own artwork for him to look at. They brought their children to watch him paint. Wherever he set up his easel, people knew him and stopped to chat. Drivers gave him a thumbs-up from the window of their cars. Sometimes someone pointed out something that Stu had neglected to put in his painting, or they told him about a building in their neighborhood that would be perfect for him to paint.

Once, when he'd set up his easel in a wooded area so he could paint a decaying school, four black teenagers ran into the woods behind the school followed by two policemen with their pistols drawn. Stu told me later that his only thought was, "I hope they don't shoot through my painting." Urban plein air painting also has its risks.

Stu hoped to show his work in an area community center or some other place where the people of Arbor Hill and West Hill could see all the paintings together. It didn't happen. However, Stu never gives up. He had noticed the magnificent Saint Joseph's Catholic Church on the outskirts of Arbor Hill and thought it would be a great place to display his paintings, but it had been abandoned for the last three decades.

About a year after he finished painting in the area, Stu made inquiries at the Ten Broeck Mansion, which was directly across the street from Saint Joseph's. He thought it might be the old church's office. It wasn't. However, the 18th century mansion had a gallery of its own. The director offered him an exhibit the following month. Stu put up posters all over the neighborhoods, inviting the community to the opening reception. It was a wonderful exhibit, a lot of people attended, but the only black people who came to see it were two Skidmore graduates.

Two years after his show at the Ten Broek Mansion in Albany, someone told Stu about the Hamilton Hill Art Center in Schenectady. He hadn't heard of it before, but the next day he brought photographs of his Arbor Hill and West Hill paintings to the director who offered him a show two weeks later. One of the Hamilton Hill Art Center's missions is to provide a place where black artists can exhibit their work in their own community, but this time they made an exception. For the next two weeks Stu completed seven paintings of Hamilton Hill so he could include them in the exhibit.

The opening reception was great. The people, mostly from the neighborhood, had asked the best questions I'd ever heard during and after Stu's talk about the exhibit. Many had seen him painting on their streets.

"Do you consider the whole outdoors your studio?", one woman asked. I told Stu he could include some of those great questions in his lectures.

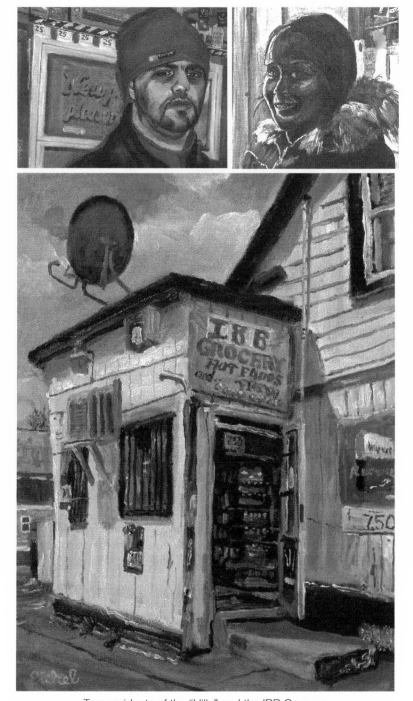

Two residents of the "Hills" and the IBB Grocery.

A few months after the show was over, the director of the Hamilton Hill Art Center asked Stu if he could bring his paintings back for an exhibit on their African-American Family Day. After all, he was an artist who'd actually painted the faces and places where the people of the neighborhood lived.

The "Newest Pizza" and the "Best Hot Dogs" in Hamilton Hill.

Stu's Saturn Sinking

Stu took this photo as soon
as he got out of the car before
his Saturn sank any further.

*People who have Saturn rising at birth
tend to want to be in control.*
Penny Thornton

On a late-September morning in 2007, Stu parked his Saturn in quicksand. He loves to create paintings of wrecked cars, trucks that will never see blacktop again, rusting farm machinery—any metal that is oxidizing to its beautiful, natural colors.

When Stu first learned about Ron Macneil's "County Auto Recycling" near Greenwich, he was ecstatic, but it took him a while to find it. Not visible from the road, the twenty-nine acre lot was filled with *hundreds* of old cars and trucks. There was so much great stuff on Ron's land that Stu thought he could probably paint there forever. However, I don't think he wanted to *die* there.

Left: A portrait of a wrecked truck. Right: A portrait of Ron Macneil.

The first time Stu showed up at "County Auto Recycling," a car blocked the entrance. Ron explained that he was in the business of selling unavailable parts for old cars and trucks and sometimes people sneaked onto his land to steal them. So Stu always called to let Ron Macneil know when he was coming, and Ron would move the car blocking the driveway. Ron did tell Stu, on the very first day, to stay on the gravel road because the ground was extremely swampy. Stu always gave Ron a print of every painting he did on his land. They became friends. Stu had been painting Ron Macneil's old cars and trucks for almost two years and Ron had gotten used to his being there.

The morning Stu drove into the quicksand, he was concentrating on finding just the right subject for his painting; some old car or decomposing truck. As he felt his car start to sink, Stu thought his last words might be "glug, glug," but he managed to get out and snap a photo of his 1994 Saturn in case he needed something to remember it by.

At the time, Stu didn't know that two years later General Motors would declare bankruptcy and Saturn would cease to exist. On March 16, 2009 a headline would read: *Saturn: GM's orphan fights for life! Abandoned and facing death as General Motors cuts brands in its own fight for survival.*

Stu's Saturn was not *abandoned* in the swamp but fighting for its life. Stu called Ron from his cell phone and asked for help. When he saw Stu's car, Ron cocked his head in amazement and told him that he had parked in quicksand. He patted Stu's shoulder and said not to worry—the pit wasn't deep enough to swallow the car. Ron was just then leaving on a business call, but he said he would try to pull the car out when he returned. Stu might just as well go ahead and paint his picture.

By the time Ron got back, Stu's painting of a car reflected in a puddle was almost finished. Ron tried to pull the Saturn out with a chain attached to the back of his truck, but was unsuccessful. So he called AAA and waited on the street for the tow truck to arrive. At first the driver absolutely refused to risk going onto that marshy land, but Ron talked him into it.

The spunky little Saturn started right up after being rescued and seemed none the worse for its near-death experience. After going to the carwash, Stu's Saturn was still covered with streaks of paint—but not quicksand. Stu told me the story after dinner. Unlike Ron Macneil, I didn't cock my head in amazement. I laughed. To me, it was business as usual.

That wonderful car had been *mine* since 1994. I'd bought it from Saturn of Knoxville at the unbelievably high price of almost $20,000 the year before I quit my job, having no idea that I was soon going to take early retirement. I *loved* that car. It was a sporty little two-door sedan with tan leather seats. It looked *nothing* like the "Dee-troit Arn" (what people from Knoxville called cars from the "Motor City") that I had always driven before.

I chose the Saturn not just for its sporty look, but because it was the first car ever to be manufactured in Tennessee. Since I was paid by the state for the twenty-five years I worked at UT, I thought it would be fitting not only to buy a car made locally, but because the sales tax would go to the state that paid my salary and then eventually would pay for my pension.

After we had moved to Saratoga Springs in 2000, we flew for our final time, back to Knoxville and drove the Saturn a thousand miles north to its new home. In 2009 Stu bought a new Honda Civic. But he couldn't bear the thought of getting oil paint all over a brand new car, so we switched cars and the license plate that was on Stu's 2006 Honda Accord now belonged to me.

I truly didn't *want* to drive a car with a license plate reading RUN STU, even though I realized that it was my job description. I wanted to keep the car that I was used to driving. However Stu now drove *my* Saturn. The sleek white exterior was quickly smeared with oil paint and the tan leather upholstery was soon streaked with the various colors of the rainbow. The inside smelled of oils and that particularly dreadful stink of turpentine. Stu loved driving that sporty little car, but I would not ever sit in it again.

During the two years that Stu drove the Saturn, he alternated between painting old cars and trucks rusting and resting at Ron Macneil's lot in Greenwich, ready and willing to give up their parts to the needy, and cars that were just sitting around and waiting for the jaws of death at 'Johnson's Auto Crushers' on Ballard Road in Wilton. Ed Johnson crushed cars that wouldn't ever again be able to compete in a demolition derby, cars that had been totaled in road accidents, or cars that had simply died of old age. Stu said after a car was crushed it could practically fit into a paper grocery bag. The people who worked at 'Johnson's Auto Crushers' were very nice to Stu, but had asked him to please always let them know where he'd parked the Saturn when he was there. They didn't want to crush it by mistake.

In 2009, when our fifteen-year-old Saturn died of old age, Stu bought a new Honda Civic at Saratoga Honda. The salesman told us he would be willing to give us $1,000 off the sticker price for the trade-in. Stu then told him that he had just put brand new tires on that Saturn (not saying that it was over his wife's very vocal objections).

The salesman rolled his eyes back in his head, and said: "That $1,000 was just out of the kindness of my heart, because that car is going straight to the crusher."

Stu's eyes filled with tears. He could not imagine that spunky little Saturn being swallowed by the jaws of death.

Stu's Mother

Elizabeth was eighty-four when she allowed
her son to paint her as "Whistler's Mother."
"I don't like it," she said. "I'm an active person.
I don't just sit around like that."

*"'Elizabeth Eichelbaum, at age ninety
the oldest person in the world to earn a Doctorate,
has never waited around. The pace of her life is nonstop.
She's an inspiration to everyone that knows her,
and her story is one of determination,
talent, and hard work."*

Believing in Ourselves: A Celebration of Women
by Nancy Carson

The last time I saw Stu's mother was the day after Thanksgiving 2002. Elizabeth died of lung cancer two months afterwards. She was almost ninety-three years old and virtually blind from macular degeneration, but that day she was cheerful and happy. Her entire family had gathered in Savannah Georgia, at her middle son Marvin's house, where she was signing the flyleaf of a recently published book, *Believing in Ourselves*, telling Elizabeth's story and the life stories of thirty-four other remarkable women.

As she was signing the copy for Stu and me, I asked her to write: "I love Greta more than Stu." She gave me a knowing little smile and signed the message below:

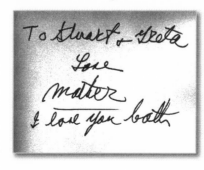

MEETING ELIZABETH

The first time I hugged my mother-in-law to be, I felt her spine stiffen, and it shocked me because I came from a family of huggers. It took me a while to realize that she had built a wall around herself. When I was twenty, the year after Stu and I had married, Elizabeth began to tell me about her childhood and started to cry. She never spoke of it to me again until she was almost seventy. I would not see her cry again until her sister Zeena died. She did not cry at her husband's funeral.

Elizabeth had the most incredible energy I had ever seen—excluding her son Stuart. She walked very fast, always wearing high heels. She drove much too fast and ate so fast that she was (annoyingly) washing the pots and pans before her guests had finished their salads. I wasn't able to keep up with her when I was eighteen and she was forty-six, and I couldn't keep up with her when she was ninety.

Elizabeth was sixty-nine years old when she became the oldest person to graduate from Wayne State since the university was founded in 1868. Her sister, Zeena, told some of their family's history to the *Detroit News*. Only then did I learn about her traumatic childhood.

THE ORPHANAGE

The youngest of three daughters, Stu's mother was born in the city of Odessa in the Ukraine on March 15, 1910. Elizabeth Shapiro was eighteen-months-old, when her father died (or disappeared) and her mother went to America, hoping to send for her daughters when she was settled and had saved enough money.

She'd left the three girls in the care of their elderly grandmother. Then the First World War broke out and not long after that, the Russian Revolution began. Their grandmother had died of starvation and the girls were placed in two different orphanages. There was little to eat and they shivered in the dark as German bombs fell.

It took ten years for their mother to find out where they were; she hired an agent to smuggle her children out of the country. She'd remarried and had a stepson just two years older than Ethel, her eldest daughter.

TELLING HER OWN STORY AT LAST

Elizabeth began writing down her memories when she was in her early seventies—she had never talked about her own life to her sons—her sisters were the only ones who knew their history. Eventually, Stu's mother gave me her stories and asked if I wanted to read them. They were amazing. I designed two slim volumes, then had Kinko's print a hundred copies of each and gave them to her at Thanksgiving. She didn't write any more about herself after that. I think she lost interest and had other things to do.

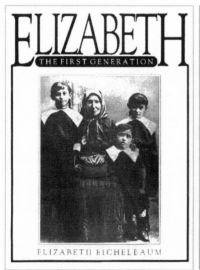 

Left: The three sisters and their grandmother. Right: Elizabeth at seventeen.

PAINTING AFTER MIDNIGHT

Elizabeth began drawing when she was eleven, soon after she came to America. Leaving school at fourteen, she worked in both a dress shop and her family's candy store, leaving little time to develop her art.

Her parents sold their candy store in New York and bought a restaurant in Detroit. A few years later they moved back to New York, opened another candy store where Elizabeth met her future husband. Martin came in every day, sat at the lunch counter, and ate nothing but ice cream. (Stu could live on ice cream.)

169

Elizabeth married Martin Eichelbaum in 1931 and gave birth to twin boys in 1932. She and Martin left New York, moving to Detroit after they had bought The Bagel Restaurant & Delicatessen. Stuart and Edward were then three-years-old. Two more sons, Marvin and Stanley, were born in Detroit. Elizabeth returned from working in the family's restaurant at around midnight set up an easel in her kitchen and started painting. Stu's father would get home about five in the morning after closing The Bagel at four. Elizabeth worked on her paintings for three to four hours each night. She would sleep until nine and then head downtown to work the lunch shift. Her oldest sister, Ethel, opened the Bagel for breakfast at 7:00 A.M.

FOUR YEARS OF GRADE SCHOOL

"I felt bad when I had no education," said Elizabeth. "I had people I met who'd ask me what university I went to, when I didn't even have more than four years of grade school."

Elizabeth came to America in 1921 and entered fifth grade. Her formal schooling abruptly ended when she was fourteen because she was required to work. High school was beyond her reach. After her husband died, Elizabeth sold Tshe Bagel and told her youngest son Stanley, "I'm going to high school." He suggested she take the test for a Graduate Equivalency Diploma and go to college instead. Elizabeth passed and got her GED in 1975, when she was sixty-five.

Stu never thought his mother was college material. He told me she had never been intellectually curious and hardly ever read a book. I asked him when did she ever have time to do anything but work? For her generation wasn't it about *surviving*? That whatever his mother decided to do really wasn't any of his business. I thought she was incredible.

GOING BACK TO SCHOOL

After getting her GED, Elizabeth added four more degrees to her four years in grade school. At Wayne State in Detroit she earned a BFA (Bachelor of Fine

Arts) in 1979 and then a Master's degree in Educational Psychology, with a specialty in Art Therapy in 1991. After moving to Tennessee, she earned an Ed.S degree (Specialist in Education) in 1995, and then an Ed.D (Doctor of Education) at the University of Tennessee in 2000. Her sons gave her a graduation party for each degree.

Elizabeth and I celebrate her Master's Degree.

ELIZABETH WANTS A JOB

After getting her Master's degree, Elizabeth wanted a job as an Art Therapist, working with people while still creating art. But it wasn't easy to get a job because of her age—eighty-one. That made her angry because she told me she could pass for seventy, but in truth she could pass for sixty. She was slender and agile; her face pretty and animated; her brown eyes intense; her thick black hair had only a touch of gray.

She volunteered at a nursing home in Detroit, giving art therapy to patients much younger than she. Later, when she volunteered at a Detroit mental hospital, she was able to induce a forty-five year old man, who had not said a word to anyone in years, to speak. She gave art therapy to mentally ill children. However, Elizabeth wanted a job that paid a salary.

It would not happen. Elizabeth had survived years in an orphanage, a year getting to America after being smuggled out of the Soviet Union with her sisters, and had worked full-time for the next fifty years. Her new job as a student would be the one she loved most, and, this job would last for the next twenty-five years.

After Martin died, Elizabeth moved out of the city of Detroit to Southfield, a suburb, but she always drove into downtown Detroit for her night classes, even when car hijackings, purse snatchings, muggings, and murders happened almost daily in the area right around Wayne State.

She had applied to Wayne to study for a Doctorate, but an official told her they had a policy that people who had received their undergraduate and master's degrees at Wayne State needed to go to another university for a doctorate. All four of her sons wanted her to move out of the Detroit area, but she refused. She had lived there for almost seventy years and it was her home.

ELIZABETH MOVES TO KNOXVILLE

Stu's mother finally decided to leave Detroit when a young woman in her neighborhood was murdered for refusing to give car-hijackers her new Mustang. When Elizabeth called and told me she was ready to get out of Detroit, I asked her if she wanted to live in Knoxville. I told her it was a nice, safe city and maybe she could enroll at the University of Tennessee and try to get her doctorate.

I told Stu that I'd just asked his mother to come live in Knoxville. "That's good," he said. She thought it over for one day, called me back and asked Stu and me to look for an apartment for her.

Since I worked for the university I knew a lot of people who I thought could help ease Elizabeth's way in enrolling as a student there. A friend in the Graduate School told me my mother-in-law would probably run into some age discrimination. She said there were a lot of fifty-year-old people who couldn't get into the doctoral program. I said there were probably a lot of fifty-year-old people who wanted to get a doctorate, but how many eighty-one-year olds were beating down the doors?

A month before she moved to Knoxville, Elizabeth visited us to see if the condo we found for her was OK. Her youngest son Stanley had bought it for her, sight unseen. "It's a little small, but I'll learn to like it," she said. That day I showed her around the UT campus and introduced her to my friend Maxine Thompson, who had recently become the head of a new office. "The Office of Re-Entry Students" was established to help older people go back to school.

The *Knoxville News-Sentinel* wanted to do a story about this new department. A reporter from the paper came to interview Maxine the day I had introduced her to Elizabeth.

"I just met the most remarkable woman," Maxine told him. The reporter called me from Maxine's office and asked if he and a photographer could come to our house that day to interview Elizabeth and take her picture. Stu's mother was on the front page of the *Knoxville News-Sentinel* a month before moving there. After the story appeared, Maxine's phone started ringing off the wall.

Senior scholar
UT program helping 81-year-old go for doctorate

By Marti Davis
News-Sentinel staff writer

One of the first students to take advantage of a new Office of Re-Entry Students at the University of Tennessee is an 81-year-old Russian immigrant.

Elizabeth Eichelbaum is seeking her doctoral degree in education.

The office is designed to meet the needs of non-traditional students, now 17 percent of UT's student population, says Director Maxine Thompson.

Thompson, a 40-year-old single mother, doctoral student and full-time UT employee, knows first hand the struggles of adult students. Her two months of working exclusively with them has been a joy, she says.

"They are really motivated. Most are willing to sacrifice some things in the short term to get what they want in the long term."

Most of those needing Thompson's help are young parents who are seeking more education as a path to better paying jobs. They are scared and confused about issues such as parking, meal plans, class scheduling and finances.

"I've been there," says Thompson. "In a sense, I'm still there."

Most of the services needed by non-traditional students are already available on campus, Thompson says she will act as a referral service and advocate for non-traditional students.

Eichelbaum is more non-traditional than most, but no less committed, says Thompson, who helped her most senior student pick a specialty (educational psychology) and is now helping her through the application process.

Eichelbaum, who received her high school diploma when she was 69 years old, says, "Education is very important. I'd like to go as far as I can."

Eichelbaum now lives in Detroit but is moving to Knoxville to be nearer her son, artist Stuart Eichel. She has purchased a West Knoxville condominium and drove here from Detroit last week to make final arrangements before her move at the end of the month.

Last from her parents as a child, Eichelbaum and her sisters were found by family when she

Please see SCHOLAR, page A4

University of Tennessee student Elizabeth Eichelbaum is studying for her doctorate at age 81.

Patrick Murphy-Racey/News-Sentinel staff

Elizabeth In front of her oil painting, "Art Sink."

Elizabeth proved to be wonderful publicity for the university, but it wasn't great for her son. I knew Stu hated his father because he was a bully, but I thought he adored his mother. I couldn't have been more wrong. Although we had been married for thirty-five years when I asked his mother to move to Knoxville, I didn't understand that he had *never* really had a loving relationship with her.

The main reason was, she never protected him from his father—who would beat him up without a word of protest from her. Stu thought she was a rotten mother. She was always busy, but did almost nothing with her children. Elizabeth worked every day at the family restaurant and the children were mostly raised and fed by their housekeeper. Stu's parents hardly spoke a word to him or his twin brother—except to yell at them. They slapped the twins around, never hugged them, or told their sons they loved them. When he was growing up, Stu remembers being terrified the few times he sat down at the table to have dinner with his parents. If he even opened his mouth to speak, his father often turned violent—giving his son a hard smack on the back of his head.

I knew Elizabeth only from when we visited Stu's parents in Detroit or they visited us in New York and later Tennessee. I realized that I didn't know anything at all about the way Stu really felt about his mother.

After seeing her new condo, Elizabeth returned to Detroit and packed all her belongings. The day after Allied Van Lines loaded the truck, she drove fourteen hours straight from Detroit to our house in Knoxville. Three days later, the moving man from Allied Van Lines called to say the truck had arrived at her condo. I went to work, but Stu took the morning off so he could drive in front of her car and lead the way to her house.

He offered to help her unpack, but she shooed him away, telling him he'd just get in the way of the two moving men and she was the only one who could tell them where to put everything. The men spent the rest of the day moving her furniture around until she was satisfied.

As soon as they left, Elizabeth immediately set to work un-packing her clothes. By the third day, all of her dishes had found their home in her newly lined kitchen cabinets and all the artwork was hung on the walls.

THE ALARM GOES OFF

On her fifth day in Knoxville, we asked Stu's mother to join us for a lecture by an "Outsider Artist" that Stu and I were both dying to see. Elizabeth said she would love to go. Stu phoned me shortly after I got home from work and asked me to call his mother and tell her we'd pick her up at 6:45. We had to be at the lecture by 7:00. All went exactly on schedule until we were leaving her house and the horrible, deafening siren of the burglar-alarm went off.

Elizabeth's son, Stanley, insisted she have a burglar alarm put in right away. The alarm company's installer gave her the code to punch in before she left the house, but she didn't remember where she'd put it and hadn't a clue of what to do next. Stu went ballistic.

"Turn the fucking thing off," he shouted.

"If your mother knew how to turn it off she probably would," I hissed through clenched teeth. Two police cars pulled up five minutes later and Elizabeth's got to meet many of her new neighbors for the first time. The police disconnected the alarm, the neighbors went back home and we finally left for the lecture—arriving only twenty minutes late. Going out the door I put my arm around Elizabeth, who was obviously shaken after being yelled at by her son.

"Mom, you do know your son is a bit crazy," I said.

"I took this crap from my husband for more than forty years," she said, "and I don't intend to take it from my son."

I told her to try to just let it go in one ear and out the other. I later asked Stu why he hadn't been honest with me about the way he really felt about his mother. "I didn't know myself, until she'd moved here," he said.

ELIZABETH'S CAR GOES TO THE BODY SHOP

On her second week in Knoxville, Elizabeth had a fender-bender. She wanted to get it fixed, but didn't want to spend a lot of money. Stu picked her up and they took her car to a cheap body shop. The repairman gave her a good estimate and set up a date, three days later, for her to bring the car back so the fender could be hammered out and repainted.

Stu drove to her house on the appointed day so that his mother could follow him to the body shop and leave her car there to be fixed. He would then drive her home where she could wait until the fender was fixed and the paint had dried.

When Stu pulled into her driveway, he honked his horn and she came right out after punching in the code for "the stupid burglar alarm." She then sat down in the passenger seat of Stu's car, buckled up her seatbelt and they drove straight to the body shop. When they arrived they said in unison: "We forgot the car!"

They had left *her* car in her garage. Elizabeth's son had inherited some other genes besides the art gene and the energy gene.

"COMPLETELY LACKING IN DESPAIR"

Elizabeth encountered some resistance to entering the doctoral program, probably because of her age. So she applied to take courses for another degree. In May of 1995, Elizabeth graduated with an Ed.S at the age of eighty-five. She had also won the award for "Most Outstanding Student" in Educational Psychology.

At the awards-presentation dinner, her teacher and advisor, Dr. Luther Kindall, made a speech. His last line was: "Elizabeth is completely lacking in despair."

DINNER PARTIES

Elizabeth could have dinner on the table for twenty people in less than half-an-hour. After years of working in restaurants, she had no idea how to cook for just a few. She always set her table with fine china and her best silverware, tapered candles in silver candlesticks, embroidered tablecloths and napkins, and tons of food. I joked that she could feed the Salvation Army Christmas Party with less food than she'd served at her dinners. Guests left her house with packages of leftovers: matzo-ball soup; Russian cabbage soup; roasted chicken; sweet and sour meatballs; noodle pudding; stuffed cabbage; potato and spinach pancakes; chopped liver; fruit salad;

Devil's Food Cake; as well as chocolate chip cookies—all homemade. She never sat down to eat with her guests. She served all the food and always insisted on cleaning up afterward.

A ONE-WOMAN ART SHOW

Elizabeth had painted for years, but never had an exhibit of her work in an art gallery. On March 6, 1993, her second year in Knoxville, she had a solo show of her paintings at the New Prospect Art Center.

Trusting no one to do it as well as she could, she hung all the paintings herself. She also prepared the food for the opening reception and stood talking to people all afternoon—wearing high heels, of course.

Many people in her family and lots of her friends traveled to Knoxville from all over the country to see the show. She never sat down for the entire three hours. That evening she gave a dinner party for forty people. Exhausted from standing around in my sneakers all afternoon, I went home to take a nap before her party.

The New Prospect Craft Center Gallery in the Candy Factory on Saturday will open an exhibit of paintings and mixed-media works by New Knoxville resident Elizabeth Eichelbaum, formerly of Detroit. A reception is scheduled for 2 to 5 p.m. Saturday in the second-floor gallery.

The Knoxville News-Sentinel announces Elizabeth's art show.

DINNER WITH ELIZABETH

Stu and I took Elizabeth out to dinner with various friends of ours almost every Sunday night. Stu's mother had always appeared streetwise to me, but her naiveté was amazing—particularly when anyone talked about sex. One night while a group of us were having dinner at our favorite Chinese Restaurant, my rather nutty friend, Betty Jean, told the assembled group that her stepfather had once French-kissed her.

"What's a French-kiss?" Stu's mother asked to a void of complete silence. Stu rolled his eyes and helplessly held out his hands, palms-up.

"It's when someone puts their tongue in your mouth while they're kissing you," I told her.

"That's really disgusting," she said. I hoped that Stu wasn't going to choke on his Egg-Foo-Young.

At one of Elizabeth's by-then-famous dinner parties, someone used the word "sodomy." I don't remember the context, but I thought: *Not really a great subject for the dinner table*. "What's sodomy?" Elizabeth asked.

"Mom, if you can't deal with French-kissing, you don't want to hear about sodomy," I replied. Somebody immediately changed the subject.

We took Elizabeth with us almost everywhere we went: to movies and plays, the ballet and once to a Klezmer concert. A friend of ours was the director of the band. Klezmer music originated in the villages and ghettos of Eastern Europe and expresses a gamut of emotions. Almost everyone in the audience was either clapping their hands or dancing in the aisles. Elizabeth sat stone-faced for the entire concert and immediately left as soon as it was over.

I later asked her if she didn't enjoy the concert. She replied, "That music brought me right back to my childhood, and I thought I'd break down and cry."

I told Stu what his mother had said and asked him why he couldn't understand that her grim childhood had forced her to keep her emotions hidden.

"I do understand," he replied, "but that doesn't make *my* childhood one bit better."

THE MIDDLE CHILD

Marvin was born six years after Stu and Eddie. One of them was often asked to look after their little brother when their mother went out. One day when Marvin was about three, it was Stu's turn to babysit. Elizabeth told her son she'd be gone for quite a while and promised to buy him a comic book for watching Marvin while she went shopping.

Stu became so involved in the book he was reading, that by the time his mother arrived home, Marvin was nowhere to be found. Elizabeth finally called the police, who eventually found Marvin about two miles from the house where he had happily wandered.

Stu said the worst part was *before* the police had found Marvin he'd asked his mother if he would still get the comic book and she slapped him silly.

EX-LAX IS NOT CANDY

Marvin would eat just about anything—especially if it looked and tasted like chocolate. Stu was once again babysitting Marvin and offered his five-year-old brother a snack of Ex-Lax. Stu knew it was medicine, although he had never tried it himself. By the time Elizabeth arrived home Marvin could not leave the bathroom. Stu's mother didn't think it was at all funny and gave him a good spanking.

MARVIN & THE MUMMY

For Thanksgiving 2010, Stu's family met for their annual get-together. It would also be a celebration of his brother Marvin's, and his wife Marilyn's 50th Wedding Anniversary. Six months before Thanksgiving, Marvin's son, Dennis, had contacted everybody in the family and asked if they would send him a funny story about Marvin. Dennis was then going to put them all in a book that he would present to his parents at their anniversary party. Stu wrote *and* illustrated his contribution, but he never heard a word from Dennis. So he called his youngest brother Stanley, and asked him if he knew whether or not Dennis had gotten a lot of submissions. Stanley told him the project had been scrapped because Stu was the *only* one to send a story to Dennis. Nobody else could remember anything funny about Marvin. So Stu framed his story (below) and gave it to Marvin at the 50th Wedding Anniversary party the night before Thanksgiving. Marvin didn't even laugh.

Mommy & Mummy

"We were in Rochester, Minnesota, where the Mayo Clinic saved my father's life. They cured his bleeding ulcer by removing one-third of his stomach. I was pulled out of school to babysit Marvin, who was six years old. That left my mother free to be at the hospital with my father. She always took Stanley, who was an infant, with her.

Marvin and I were parked in the city's most ancient hotel. We had to use a communal bathroom down the hall because our room didn't have a toilet.

I would leave the room with the used bedsheets. In the hall I would wrap them around me to create a poor-man's version of the mummy, the most terrifying monster of the horrow films I feared but loved. When Marvin answered my knock at the door it achieved the desired effect.

But, in the end, Marvin won. Rather than enter the hall where the monster roamed, he peed in our room. Urine in the wastebasket was my undoing. Mother slapped the mummy silly. Mummies didn't scare her. At least not this mummy. I was shortly packed off to Detroit to continue my schooling. I never got to do my next production . . . The Revenge of the Mummy."

THREE BIRTHDAYS

Stuart, Edward and their youngest brother Stanley were all born on June 8th. Elizabeth gave a party for all three of them when her eldest sons turned sixty. Stan, the youngest June 8th baby by thirteen years, produced three tee-shirts. Stu's said, "I'm not Eddie," Eddie's, of course, "I'm not Stu," and Stan's, "Can you believe I have 60 year-old brothers?" I always joked that the middle brother, Marvin, born on October 3rd must have been conceived in a drunken fit of passion. If you knew their parents, you'd understand the joke.

ANOTHER GRADUATION DAY

Left to right: Edward, Marvin, Elizabeth, Stan and Stu.

3,202 students graduated on May 12, 2000 at the Thompson/Boling Arena. The huge arena, used for the University of Tennessee's basketball games, had a full house of almost 25,000 people. Elizabeth stole the show. Both of my children had graduated from UT, so I knew it was going to be a *very* long day, and I knew the drill.

Each undergraduate's name is called before he or she walks very quickly across the stage, is handed a rolled up piece of paper and shakes the hand of the Dean of his or her college. (They pick up their real degrees the next day.) The audience is asked not to applaud until after they are seated. The guests then only clap for their own undergraduate. It is truly an unutterably boring day. I made it through my own children's graduation only because I was a lot younger then.

The Master's and Doctoral students are introduced one at a time. The University of Tennessee has nine undergraduate colleges and eleven graduate colleges. The Master's and Doctoral students and their guests in the audience also clap only for the graduates of their own college.

When Elizabeth went on stage to accept her degree, Dr. Joseph Johnson, the President of UT, asked her if she minded if he told her age. After Dr. Johnson handed her the doctoral degree and gave her a hug, every single college and every person in the audience gave her a standing ovation. "What do you think now, Mr. Smarty Pants?" I asked Stu. Elizabeth was glowing—loving every minute of the attention she must have always craved.

Elizabeth was later flown from Knoxville to New York to be on "Good Morning America," and *The New York Times* published a story about her life and accomplishments. She received a letter from the White House signed by Bill Clinton congratulating her for her accomplishments.

ELIZABETH'S FINAL STORY IN THE KNOXVILLE NEWS-SENTINEL

The University of Tennessee sent out a press release about Elizabeth's death. *The Knoxville News-Sentinel* called two of her professors and asked if they wanted to say something that the newspaper could use in her obituary.

Elizabeth Eichelbaum, who earned doctorate at 90, dies

News-Sentinel staff

A former Knoxville resident who inspired others to further their education by earning a doctorate degree at age 90 died Wednesday at her home in Savannah, Ga., according to University of Tennessee officials.

Elizabeth Eichelbaum, 92, was an artist and art therapist whose achievements were noted in the New York Times and who once appeared as a guest on "Good Morning America," a UT press release stated.

"I have never experienced anyone with such drive and determination," said professor Thomas N. Turner, Mrs. Eichelbaum's adviser in the UT College of Education.

"What Elizabeth set out to do, she would do, and nothing—not age, not disease, not the obstructionism of people who [view] age as a handicap—would ever stop her. She was indomitable."

Retired professor Luther Kindall also remembered Mrs. Eichelbaum. "She was the most inspirational student I ever taught. I was her mentor, but she was really a mentor to me."

Mrs. Eichelbaum was born in Russia in 1910 and survived a "grim childhood and a yearlong journey to America" to arrive in New York at the age of 11. She left school after the eighth grade to work but dreamed of continuing her education. For the next five years, she raised

four children and built a restaurant business in Detroit with her husband.

At 69, she received a B.A. in fine arts from Wayne State University, followed by an M.A. in art history from Oakland University at age 80. She then moved to Knoxville and began working as an art therapist for the elderly and mentally handicapped. While in Knoxville, she decided to start work on a doctorate.

When she graduated her family established a scholarship in her name at UT for graduate students returning to study after at least a 10-year absence.

She is survived by four sons, four grandchildren and 10 great-grandchildren.

"I have never experienced anyone with such drive and determination," said professor Thomas Turner, her advisor at the College of Education. "What Elizabeth set out to do she would do—not age, not disease, not the obstructionism of people who view age as a handicap—would ever stop her. She was indomitable." Retired professor Luther Kindall also remembered Mrs. Eichelbaum: "She was the most inspirational person I ever taught. I was her mentor, but she was really a mentor to me."

I remember Stu's mother's eternal optimism. When it was raining cats and dogs she'd say: "The sun will be out soon." When a war was being fought; "It will end." When you thought you wouldn't be able to walk: "Don't worry, I promise you'll walk again." When the children got sick: "They will get better."

And I'll never forget the words Dr. Luther Kindall spoke when she won the prize for outstanding student: "Elizabeth is completely lacking in despair." Those words truly defined her

Elizabeth wanted to be buried in Detroit next to her husband. The burial was held on a cold, cloudy day in early February. Stu and I came back one year later for the unveiling of her tombstone. The sun was shining. Engraved on the stone:

DR. ELIZABETH EICHELBAUM
BORN MARCH 15, 1910
DIED JANUARY 28, 2003.

SETTING A WORLD RECORD

In 2004 the *Guinness Book of World Records* gave the title: "The oldest person in the world to earn a Doctorate to American Elizabeth Eichelbaum."

The book came out one year after she died. She would have loved being in the *Guinness Book of World Records*, although I don't think she would have liked the idea of any person getting a title for spending the longest amount of time sitting on top of a telephone pole.

I can almost hear her saying: "Why would someone want to sit on top of a telephone pole when they could be out doing something?"

Stu Doodles

Stu doodled since childhood and still does.

*Doodling is drawing aimlessly
or absent-mindedly usually while doing
something else, such as having a telephone
conversation or attending a meeting.*

In 1963, mathematician Stanislaw Ulam developed the Ulam spiral for the visualization of prime numbers while he was doodling during a boring presentation at a mathematics conference. In 2012, Stu doodled the above during a meeting of the Guild of Adirondack Artists.

Although Stanislaw Ulam ultimately received great acclaim for doodling an important mental picture, Stu (who flunked math) told me that if anybody at the Adirondack Artist's meeting had noticed his doodle, in all likelihood they would not have invited him to come back. Stu's "mental" picture might have prompted some other artist to summon the guys with the white coats and the nets.

DOODLERS

Many of the American Presidents, including Thomas Jefferson, Ronald Reagan, and Bill Clinton, have been known to doodle during meetings. Poet and physician John Keats doodled in the margins of his medical notes.

According to a study published in the scientific journal *Applied Cognitive Psychology*, doodling can aid a person's memory. The act of doodling expends just enough energy to keep one from daydreaming and helps the doodler to pay more attention to what he or she is trying to listen to. It helps the doodler *focus* on the current situation.

That analysis certainly applies to Stu. His doodling is truly an out-of-body experience. When he hangs up the phone he is always surprised that he can tell how annoying the phone call had been by the doodle. He looks at it as if for the first time. He never remembers the act of drawing it.

NO SAFE PLACE

No blank or partially written on piece of paper like a shopping list, is safe from Stu's doodles. We add to our list when we run out of important staples like Cool Whip or Saran Wrap.

One list shoots me a bird. I'll start a list *under* a doodle and find arms wrapped around it. I start another list copying the few items only to find he's added cookies and a doodle letting me know he's baaaack. When I needed sliced almonds, I simply taped one of the kind I wanted to the list. It made a perfect mouth to doodle around. I made a list too long for Stu to do a decent doodle and I felt sorry for the little guy scrunched up on the bottom realizing he's fucked. And then he handed me his "List Ultimatum," as if it was my idea to save his doodles for our grandkids.

DOODLING AROUND AT THE MARRIOTT

Whenever we visit our granddaughters and their parents in Winchester, Massachusetts, we stay at the Burlington Marriott. We stay for a day or two and then drive the five hours back home. Stu and I are too old to be grandparents of young children. We adore the girls, who are now ten and eight-years-old, but my energy is totally drained after four or five hours. Even "Stu the Energizer Bunny," gets tired.

We get up earlier than usual for the drive home so Stu will have enough time after we return to run his usual six-miles. While I'm getting ready to leave, he doodles on the Marriott notepad, which suggests: "Leave a trail of genius" which he does with the Marriott pen, so I can appreciate how long I have kept him waiting. Sometimes he doodles ugly princesses.

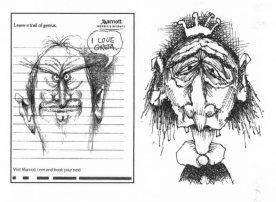

DOODLING UGLY PRINCESSES

When our granddaughters were in their "Princess" phase, each parading around the house wearing long crepe-paper gowns and crowns on their heads, Stu began doodling ugly princesses for them. He would say how beautiful his princesses were and they would tell him they were ugly and tear them into small pieces. Before they understood the joke they couldn't imagine why their Grandpa, who was such a good artist, could think his princesses were beautiful. Jordana, when she was four, asked him if it was true that he went to school to learn to draw ugly princesses. "Who told you that?" he asked.

"Grandma Greta," she said.

187

For Michaela's ninth birthday, August 4, 2012, Stu created two oil paintings. The birthday girl had her choice of which princess she wanted. She picked the painting labeled "beautiful princess" over the painting labeled "ugly witch." Stu said: "She gets it."

For Jordana's seventh birthday on September 21, 2012, she got to choose which one of her Grandpa's two ugly princess paintings *she* wanted to hang in her room. I am waiting for her to say, "None of the above."

Stu now takes as much pleasure in creating his ugly princesses as he does painting landscapes, cityscapes, rusting cars, ancient trucks, old tractors, or anything else that he has been painting for the last twenty years.

I designed a calendar for 2013 using all of Stu's ugly princesses. He'd become so in love with painting them we realized that we probably couldn't *live* long enough to give them all those princesses to our granddaughters for their birthdays.

Fortunately, there is always inheritance.

Stu Does Not Compute

Stu doodled the above while talking
to technical help about
a problem with his computer.

"Attitude is a little thing that makes
a big difference. It either leads to having a positive
or negative effect on the relationship."
Winston Churchill

Winston Churchill was right. A bad attitude has a negative effect on a relationship. In the fifty-six years that Stu and I have been married, the only time we've come close to getting divorced is when I've tried to teach him something on his computer. I immediately become the enemy.

A BAD ATTITUDE

From the first day he entered kindergarten, a lot of Stu's teachers regularly asked his parents to come to school to discuss their son's bad behavior. He stayed in trouble throughout elementary school, and even his high school principal sometimes felt it necessary to call his parents. Stu's commanding officer in the army didn't call his parents—the U.S. Army has its own way of dealing with a bad attitude.

IT'S GOOD TO BE KING

During the last twenty-five years of his advertising career, Stu was the boss. When he was creative director at two different ad agencies, the personal computer didn't yet exist. By the time computers became essential, he was a partner in Reed/Eichel Advertising and had "computer slaves." He *could* have learned to use a computer himself then, but one thought stopped him: *it's good to be king*. Stu left advertising in 1991 and has been a full-time artist ever since.

I retired in 1995. For the last ten years of my career as a graphic designer at The University of Tennessee, I learned everything I needed to know about designing on the Mac. I bought my own MacPlus, a very early version of the Apple, so I could "learn more by doing" at home— it's really the only way to learn I told Stu. He showed no interest.

I AM NOT YOUR COMPUTER SLAVE

After we moved to Saratoga Springs, Stu started organizing exhibits of his paintings. He then needed someone to design and print posters, invitations, and his various 'artist statements.' That *someone* was not going to be me. He bought his own Apple laptop, a scanner, and a printer. He took a free class offered by the Saratoga Springs Public Library, but the instructor told him he was hopeless. He was not really *hopeless*, but someone who truly loved him was going to have to teach him.

STU LEARNS (SORT OF)

If his studio were on the second floor of our house, where *I* work, instead of in the basement, Stu would have thrown his laptop out the window the first time it betrayed him. He considers any computer problem to be a *personal* betrayal. Maybe he's right. There is not a mechanical device on the planet that he gets along with. Stu hates them all. If they were *human* and capable of emotion they would hate him as well. Sometimes he actually punches his computer. Once when a stubborn CD refused to eject, he tried forcing the disk out with a screwdriver. I told him, "That's what is called screwing yourself."

I try to avoid going down two flights of stairs when I hear the sound of Stu screaming, "Motherfucker." I can clearly hear his fury through the air-conditioner vents or when the windows are open. After the fourth or fifth howling of "Motherfucker," I usually go down to the basement to help him, but only because I'm afraid even the neighbors might hear him and call the police.

In truth, Stu is a terrible student and I am a terrible teacher. A good teacher wouldn't start a lesson with: "You fucking moron." Stu has no patience listening to *anyone* trying to explain what will and will not work on the computer. However, when I'm not home and he gets desperate for help, he calls technical assistance. Then he leaves notes to make me feel guilty.

WHEN PIGS FLY

"When Pigs Fly" is a way of saying that something will never happen. It is used to scoff at over-ambition. Whenever I try to teach Stu how to create something new on his computer, I'm not sure which one of us is the pig. I always believe I can't teach him and he always believes he can't learn. Stu still leaves his "helpless" doodles around so I will take pity on him.

I used to have to start from scratch with my lesson whenever Stu needed a new poster, invitation, or artist statement. But it's true when they say that one should never say "never" or scoff at over-ambition. Stu can now create posters and everything else he needs all by himself on his Apple laptop and print them on his HP Deskjet. Congratulations are due to both the teacher and her student.

"HEY LOOK! THERE GOES A FLYING PIG!"

192

About Face

PORTRAITS FROM THE MIND OF STU EICHEL

Stu's About Face

In the winter of 2013, Stu went
in a different direction.

*"There have always been strange beings
lurking in my head. I doodle them with a pencil while
talking on the phone or eating. My wife thought these doodles
were fun so she saved them in a folder."*

Stu Eichel

Ed Sakos is the owner of Mr. Ed's Ice Cream on Route 29 between Saratoga Springs and Schuylerville. Stu, who is addicted to ice cream, is his best customer. Ed also holds flea markets once a month next to his store. One day he said, "Hey Stu, I have a great big package for you." Stu couldn't imagine what it would be . . . a big package of what?

It turned out to be a load of art supplies that Mr. Ed had acquired on one of his many buying trips. Among the stuff was a brand new set of acrylic paints.

In almost twenty years as a fine artist Stu had never used anything other than oil paints. But he decided this was too good a deal to pass up. So he gave the acrylics a try.

Since Stu was now starting out on a new adventure, he chose to paint something from his mind rather than the usual stuff he sees outside. Mr. Ed's gift was like getting a box of gold. Last winter, he did more than one hundred goofy portraits.

During the month of April 2013, Stu had an exhibit of his face paintings at the Saratoga Arts Center. The show was such a hit that the director asked Stu if he could leave his work there for another week after the show closed. They were hosting a meeting for many of the directors of art centers in upstate New York, and he wanted them to see the exhibit.

The Arts Center also held a workshop for a group of local children. They were invited to create a painting or a drawing or anything that inspired them from looking at Stu's faces. But they asked the children to please not paint or draw the painting (above) called "The Final Cut." Their parents might object.

The exhibit, like the poster, was titled: **About Face: *Portraits from the Mind of Stu Eichel.***

A woman came up to me at the opening reception and said, "I don't think I would want to live in your husband's head." I told her that Stu and I had been married for fifty-six years, and that I probably wouldn't want to live there either. But then I thought, "Don't knock it till you've tried it." Have a good day.

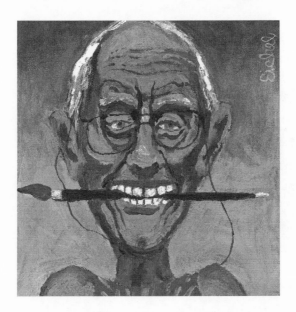

Made in the USA
Charleston, SC
20 January 2014